Second Edition

Performance-Based Learning

To my sister
Mary Anne Snyder,
a model performance learner

Second Edition

Performance-Based Learning

Aligning Experiential Tasks and Assessment to Increase Learning

Sally Berman

Second Edition of
Performance Based Learning for the Multiple Intelligences Classroom

CORWIN PRESS
A SAGE Publications Company
Thousand Oaks, CA 91320

For information:

Corwin Press
A Sage Publications Company
2455 Teller Road
Thousand Oaks, California 91320
www.corwinpress.com

Sage Publications Ltd.
1 Oliver's Yard
55 City Road
London EC1Y 1SP
United Kingdom

Sage Publications India Pvt. Ltd.
B 1/I 1 Mohan Cooperative
    Industrial Area
Mathura Road, New Delhi 110 044
India

Sage Publications Asia-Pacific Pte. Ltd.
33 Pekin Street #02-01
Far East Square
Singapore 048763

Printed in the United States of America.

Library of Congress Cataloging-in-Publication Data

Berman, Sally.
Performance-based learning: Aligning experiential tasks and assessment to increase learning/Sally Berman.—2nd ed.
    p. cm.
Includes bibliographical references and index.
ISBN 978-1-4129-5309-2 (cloth : alk. paper)
ISBN 978-1-4129-5310-8 (pbk. : alk. paper)
    1. Competency based education—United States. I. Title.

LC1032.B46 2008
371.39—dc22   2006102776

This book is printed on acid-free paper.

08 09 10 11 12 10 9 8 7 6 5 4 3 2 1

Acquisitions Editor:	Cathy Hernandez
Editorial Assistant:	Megan Bedell
Production Editor:	Sarah K. Quesenberry
Copy Editor:	Cate Huisman
Typesetter:	C&M Digitals (P) Ltd.
Proofreader:	Gail Fay
Indexer:	Molly Hall
Cover Designer:	Lisa Riley

Contents

Preface

For the past several years, classroom teachers and assessment authorities have extolled the benefits of performance assessment. As students show what they know by doing a performance or task, teachers see more clearly what students have mastered and what learning has eluded them. Good teachers use the results of performance assessments to improve the learning experiences that students encounter in their classrooms. Caring teachers say, "If we expect students to do a task or performance to demonstrate their learning, we need to make learning contextual. We want the learning experiences to align with the assessment techniques."

These teachers construct communities of active learners in their classrooms. They invite students to become partners by explaining the learning standards that students are expected to meet, giving students rubrics that describe developmental levels of performance, and showing students how to use the rubrics to evaluate the strengths of their present performances, decide how to improve those performances, and work toward that improvement. In these classrooms, students learn the life-long skill of *kaizen*, the use of continual self-assessment, adjustment, and stepwise improvement to achieve high-quality results.

Performance-based learning has roots in the ideas of John Dewey. With his strong belief in the educative nature of all experience, Dewey (1916) saw doing as a way of connecting information and ideas. The work of Csikszentmihalyi (1990) on flow, the experience of being so immersed in an engaging task that one is swept along in its current, provides more current thinking on the value of experiential learning.

In 1988, Dr. Marian Diamond said that experiential learning is the key to growing the axon-dendrite connections that brains use to process cognitive information. Her studies suggest that student involvement and interaction with materials in and out of the classroom build better brains for learning. Caine and Caine (1991) stated that the brain remembers best what it learns in context. Both sets of research point to performance learning as a tool for developing deeper understanding and for enhancing ability to apply knowledge of facts appropriately in a new situation (Gardner, 1991). More recently, Keller (2004) stated that maximizing student success in school involves increasing not only rigor, but also relevance. Performance-based learning is well suited to accomplishing this difficult assignment.

Performance learning is a curriculum model that produces deep, long-lasting learning and develops expertise in procedural skills, and it can be used successfully by teachers in all grade levels, kindergarten through college, with students from all socioeconomic groups and communities.

AS YOU READ THIS BOOK

The Chapters

First, notice that the focus of this book is not performance assessment. Each activity in Chapters 2 through 10 details a learning experience that aligns with assessment. If the goal of the assessment is to have students show what they know, the goal of the activity is to experience the knowing.

Read the first chapter carefully. It contains the research base for this curriculum model, and it references the work done by many educational and brain physiology experts. The reference section at the end of the book lists these and other references. Readers are encouraged to obtain and read some of these resource materials to acquire useful tips and background information.

Browse through the rest of the chapters. Each chapter details a performance learning task that the teacher may choose to use as presented or may use as a model for developing performance learning applications of his or her own. Notice that each chapter uses the same basic outline that includes the performance, prompt, vision, standards, coaching context, presentation, and reflection.

Each chapter begins by addressing the student audience targeted by the task (*The Audience*) and includes a brief description of the performance learning task and reasons why the task fits the performance learning model (*The Performance*). The chapter goes on to describe how the teacher might present the task and to provide examples of excellent performance presentations to the students (*The Prompt*).

In each chapter, the section titled *The Vision* describes how the teacher and students can inspect examples of learning and presentation excellence. These examples of expert practices in learning and presenting will help students self-evaluate and improve the quality of their learning as they work their way through the performance task and the final presentation.

In *The Standards*, look at the task development chart. It contains the steps in the performance task, the curriculum standards that align with the task, and a description of the performance development levels from novice to expert. *The Standards* also contains the rubric for the performance learning task. This rubric can be used as a final assessment tool. Its more powerful use is for ongoing self-evaluation and performance improvement by students as they work toward the final presentation. Students who know the assessment standards, or criteria, and who have seen examples of excellent performances will demonstrate deeper understanding and more proficient learning.

The section titled *The Coaching Context* details the actions of students and teacher in the performance learning task. Each chapter concludes with a description of the presentation performance (*The Presentation*) and suggestions for individual or group reflection (*The Reflection*).

Teachers may use this book to jump-start their imaginations as they decide how students can best learn specific content. Each reader may pick one learning standard that students are expected to meet and ask, "To show that they have learned this, what will I ask students to do? What performance or task will I ask students to demonstrate?" The answer to that question can guide the teacher in structuring the classroom experience into a performance learning task.

Online Resources

Each chapter includes at least a mention of the helpfulness of Internet resources in planning and implementing performance learning tasks. Sometimes the references include specific Web sites, and most of the time they make the more general statement that a good search engine will locate many Web sites that teachers will find helpful. All Internet users know that a Web site that exists one year is often gone the next, and that is the reason for recommending a search rather than providing specific URLs.

If students use the Internet to research a topic, the teacher will want to monitor Web use carefully. Students need guidance in evaluating reliability of Web sites and their information, and teachers need to know that the sites students are using are content and age appropriate.

Learning Teams

Every activity in this book involves the use of cooperative learning teams. Teachers need to be aware of the importance of planning cooperative learning experiences to include all of the elements needed to insure successful learning by all students. Bellanca and Fogarty (2001) suggest that the acronym **BUILD** will help teachers remember those elements:

- **B**ring in higher-order thinking.
- **U**nite the teams.
- **I**nsure individual accountability.
- **L**ook back; reflect and process often.
- **D**evelop teamwork skills.

Here are a few suggestions about each element:

B: Ask students to do more than memorize facts. Aligning tasks with standards will bring in more complex ways of knowing.

U: Assign students to heterogeneous teams, and give each member of a team a specific role to play. Assigning roles carefully helps teachers address the needs of diverse students. Give each team a well-defined task, and assign a meaningful final demonstration of learning that requires every member of a team to do his or her part.

I: Give each student a meaningful personal task. This can be keeping a journal, completing a writing or sketching assignment, performing a task, demonstrating factual knowledge on a test or quiz, or self-evaluating performance and learning.

L: Ask teams to process how well they worked together as well as what they learned.

D: Brainstorm a list of protocols or teamwork rules, give teams time to practice using those skills, and monitor teams as they practice.

Teachers who are unfamiliar with using cooperative learning teams will want to research this practice. Cooperative learning is not the same as "groupwork." In a cooperative classroom, every student plays a meaningful role and contributes to the learning of all class members.

Each activity in this book suggests that teachers assign students to teams of three. Within these teams, the roles are as follows:

- **Correspondent:** This person checks with teammates for understanding and consensus, makes a written record of team ideas and answers to brainstorming questions, and reports answers to the rest of the class.
- **Conductor:** This person keeps the team on time and on task, checks for progress toward completion of the task, and directs rehearsals of performances or presentations.
- **Dry Cell:** This person encourages and energizes the team, uses appropriate humor to keep the task flowing, and monitors and directs use of teamwork skills.

In addition to having these basic jobs, each member of a team has responsibilities specific to the performance learning task. Chapter 11 in this book includes more information about and suggestions for using cooperative learning to enhance learning for all students.

What's New in the Second Edition

Updates and revisions have been made throughout the book, and each chapter includes a new section (*The Audience*) that identifies appropriate grade levels for the activity and suggests ways in which teachers can use learning teams to adapt the activity for diverse learners. Information on cooperative learning teams has been added, as has a new chapter: Chapter 11, Designing Performance Learning Activities, which contains suggestions that teachers can use to develop their own performance learning units. A new section at the end of the book includes reproducible masters that teachers can use in planning and implementing performance learning tasks.

Acknowledgments

So many influences contributed to the shaping of this book. Al, my partner and love, gave me the time, freedom, and encouragement to do these pieces of writing and understood that time spent looking out the window or walking on the beach is time I need to blow out the mental cobwebs and set off creative sparks.

For the first edition, Jean Ward and Barb Lightner at SkyLight cared for the manuscript and guided it through the publication process. Their thoughts, ideas, and expertise added immeasurably to the quality of the final product.

For this second edition, Cathy Hernandez and Megan Bedell at Corwin Press helped with suggestions, provided files and other materials, answered questions, and encouraged me with patience and good humor; Cate Huisman refined and polished the manuscript and always knew when more information was needed; and Sarah Quesenberry guided the book through production. Each of them played a vital role in making this book a quality product.

As I looked at the fit between the performance learning model and the performance tasks I was creating, I found myself integrating and coordinating research on brain growth and learning from many different sources, all of whom are listed in the reference list. Writing this book encouraged me to review work on multiple intelligences, brain growth, emotional intelligence, and experiential learning.

Internet resources are invaluable to me as a writer. The national, state, and local learning standards that I found online gave me valuable insight into the performances that policy makers expect of students in their school systems. I found Web sites with helpful information about some of the skills and information needed to do every performance task in this book, so the Internet gave me the freedom to write in the wilderness, miles from large research facilities.

Without the support and encouragement of such an extended network of people and resources, I would not have been able to write this book.

Publisher's Acknowledgments

Corwin Press gratefully acknowledges the contributions of the following reviewers:

Cathy L. Benedict, Assistant Professor
and Coordinator of Undergraduate
Music Education Studies
New York University
New York, NY

Deborah Rose Howell, Multiyear
Elementary School Teacher
Monte Cristo Elementary School
Granite Falls, WA

Rachel Moreno, Associate Professional
Specialist
University of Notre Dame
Notre Dame, IN

Masha K. Rudman, Professor of
Teacher Education and Curriculum
University of Massachusetts
Amherst, MA

Debbie Stasiw, Gifted Science and
Reading Middle School Teacher
Driftwood Middle Academy of Health
and Wellness
Hollywood, FL

Leslie Wilson, Professor of Education
University of Wisconsin
Stevens Point, WI

About the Author

Sally Berman is an experienced, creative facilitator of interactive workshops teaching educators how to create classrooms in which their students develop teamwork, cognition, metacognition, and self-evaluation skills. Sally developed and tested many of her ideas during her 30 years of science teaching at a large high school in the Chicago suburbs.

Sally received her AB in chemistry and mathematics in 1964 and her MS in chemical education in 1969. In the mid-1980s, feeling a need for professional rejuvenation, she embarked on a learning quest that led to work with a number of outstanding educators and theorists. A few of these were Jim Bellanca, David and Roger Johnson, David Lazear, Kay Burke, and Robin Fogarty.

Using her newly acquired information, Sally created and led workshops and graduate courses for a variety of clients. She has worked with educators and industrial trainers from the United States, Canada, the Netherlands, Britain, Eastern Europe, and Australia.

Sally lives with Al, her best friend and husband of 36 years, near Ontonagon, Michigan, on the south shore of Lake Superior. They met when both were teaching at Palatine High School in Palatine, Illinois. Sally says, "It was love in the lounge!" Sally taught chemistry, and Al taught English and coached wrestling. Sally does not get up in the dark; she does, on occasion, stay up until dawn. She is sometimes compared with the Kay Thompson creation, Eloise.

A Cautionary Tale

Once upon a time, a school staff decided that its highest priority was helping students to become better writers. Students spent much time analyzing sentences to identify parts of speech. They combed through long lists of sentences looking for capitalization and punctuation errors. Exercising their visual skills, students diagrammed sentences to show the relationships of the parts to the whole. Student investigators inspected sentences for subject/verb agreement, dangling participles, and split infinitives. At the end of the school year, students took a multiple-choice test to demonstrate their mastery of writing skills. Test scores were high. The school staff was pleased.

Time passed. The students graduated and moved to new schools and jobs. One by one, they heard, "Your writing is terrible! Where did you go to school? Didn't they teach you anything at that place? You need to take a remedial writing course if you want to be successful with us." The students returned to the school exclaiming, "We thought we were learning to write! But we don't know how to write! We just don't get it! You said you were teaching us how to write!"

The moral is this: Performing glues a skill in the brain; he (or she) who performs, learns.

1

Introduction to Performance Learning

WHAT IS PERFORMANCE LEARNING?

Performance learning immerses students in learning facts, skills, and concepts by doing tasks or performances. A teacher or mentor guides the learner as he or she practices and refines a skill. The learner demonstrates proficiency by doing the skill, first in familiar settings and ultimately in new situations. To celebrate success, the student displays skill development in a public performance.

Performance learning is the difference between watching a concert on television and playing an instrument as part of a band or an orchestra. The television viewer does not feel the vibration of the stage, the concussion from the percussion, or the movement necessary to play the instrument with expert skill. The novice musician feels all those things plus the internal twinge that comes from playing a wrong note or playing a note at the wrong time. Focusing on the skill keeps novices producing the notes in the correct order. As they practice and their proficiency improves, their attention shifts to the phrasing of the music and its implied emotion. They may be in the company of others each time they practice the skill. If they share the practice room with other musicians, the others may notice the novices' ongoing improvement and comment about it. The novices and the more experienced musicians share a common, informal set of standards by which they evaluate the performance. Many people who have learned to play an instrument remember the benchmarks that indicate each increase in skill development. Everyone on the stage shares a common vision of the expert playing with deep feeling during a concert with an internationally famous ensemble.

Learning to play an instrument may be linked to other, broader concepts such as the recognition that music seems to be hard wired into the human genetic code (Jensen, 2002). Novice musicians may have decided that they want to do more with music than sing in the shower or play a kazoo. A music teacher from a novice's school or a professional musician who is part of a school outreach program may have suggested that the novice learn to play an instrument, and he or she has decided to give it a try. The novices' commitment to learning to play demonstrates their understanding of the importance of music in cognitive development. By choosing to learn a new skill to apply these ideas, novices are demonstrating understanding as Gardner (1991) defines it. They are applying their knowledge of the facts appropriately in a new situation.

WHEN IS PERFORMANCE LEARNING THE MOST APPROPRIATE MODEL FOR THE LEARNING TASK?

Sometimes, the most effective learning results from doing a task or practicing a performance that applies important facts or concepts. Caine and Caine (1991) state that the brain remembers best what it learns in the context of ordinary, everyday experiences. The novice musician remembers the feelings of creativity or relaxation or alertness that were experienced in the context of listening to music and recognizes some of these same feelings when he or she produces the music. A science student who manages a compost pile with expert results learns how to manage the speed of chemical reactions. For the novice musician or scientist or learner of any other content, process, or skill, research shows that the ideas and concepts that are embedded in this kind of natural, spatial learning experience are the ones that stick to the brain.

The brain processes parts and wholes simultaneously. Too often, classroom instruction focuses on the parts and ignores the whole, and removing wholeness also removes meaning (Caine, Caine, McClintic, & Klimek, 2005). The compost-making science student's brain remembers facts about factors that affect the speed of a reaction because the brain is focused on the details of temperature, moisture, added ingredients, scrap size, and the whole picture of turning food scraps and lawn clippings into compost. The compost pile provides a context within which the details and concepts are more lastingly remembered.

In deciding when to use performance learning, teachers will want to ask themselves these questions:

- Are these ideas or concepts embedded in a particular task or performance?
- What skills are associated with learning these ideas or concepts?
- What learning do my students need to be able to demonstrate to graduate to the next level of education?

Inspecting school district or state standards will help teachers answer the last question. Information about standards can be found on a number of Web sites, including (at the time of this writing) http://www.mcrel.org/standards/benchmarks (a site maintained by the Mid-continent Research for Education and Learning organization) and http://www.education-world.com/standards (the Web site of Education World).

Most states have published criteria for graduation: standards and benchmarks that describe and define the learning that students must exhibit in order to graduate to the next learning level. These standards and benchmarks often specify that students will demonstrate their learning by doing a performance assessment. Performance learning provides students with the skills they will be asked to demonstrate on performance assessments by providing students with explicit instruction in strategies and skills (McTighe, 1996–97). When students are engaged in performance learning, learning strategies align with assessment techniques, students know how they will be expected to demonstrate learning, they frequently self-assess progress toward their goals, and they learn more (Caine et al., 2005).

WHY IS PERFORMANCE LEARNING EFFECTIVE? HOW DOES PERFORMANCE LEARNING HELP STUDENTS BECOME QUALITY LEARNERS?

As teacher and student assess performance, they begin by focusing on what the student can do and how his performance has improved since the previous assessment. The student experiences positive emotions about his task or skill development, and this enhances further learning and improvement in important ways. Ornstein and Sobel (1987) say that people want to repeat pleasant experiences and avoid unpleasant ones. O'Keefe and Nadel (1978) conclude that positive emotions create the conditions for the brain to form better cognitive maps. Caine et al. (2005) say that students who experience "relaxed alertness" are more likely to take charge of their own learning and to grow a brain that can learn more successfully. The student will be able to remember his performance more clearly, repeat it more effortlessly, and remember associated ideas and concepts more accurately when he remembers learning as a pleasant experience.

At the beginning of the task, the teacher, as a performance learning coach, and the student will look at the stages of skill development and the vision of the final level of achievement. The teacher will encourage the learner to focus on improvement and step-by-step skill development. This focus on gradual improvement is especially important for young children who often are not aware of the natural stages of skill development (Tomlinson, 1999). Depending on the children's ages, the teacher can help them understand the concept of developmental stages by asking if they remember learning another skill, for example, fastening shoes or coloring inside the lines, and the teacher and students can discuss the development stages of that performance.

To guide learners through development of the new performance, the teacher will give them a rubric that details the performance criteria for each developmental level. The coach—who can be either the teacher or a fellow student—will encourage the learner to continuously self-evaluate personal performance, determine personal developmental level, and look for improvement by asking these questions:

- What developmental criteria does my performance meet?
- What's the developmental level of my performance?
- What am I doing well?
- What's the next developmental stage?
- How can I get there?
- What do I need to improve?
- Who can help me?

This continual focus on performance improvement illustrates the Japanese principle of kaizen that is a focus of many quality management programs. Kaizen teaches that waiting until the final performance to do any evaluating of the learner's progress will not lead to a quality performance. Continual self-assessment, adjustment, and stepwise improvement are needed to build a quality performance.

Performance learning is brain-friendly learning and leads to quality because it

- Focuses on what the student can do.
- Identifies how the student's performance has improved.
- Fosters a positive emotional climate for learning.
- Identifies the next stage in skill development.
- Provides criteria for each stage in skill development.
- Provides a framework for kaizen, or continuous improvement.

WHAT ARE THE DEVELOPMENTAL STAGES IN PERFORMANCES? HOW DO WE EVALUATE PERFORMANCE LEVELS?

Skill growth in all kinds of performances seems to follow a common path. As identified by Posner and Keele (1973), the phases of skill development are novice, advanced beginner, competent user, proficient performer, and expert. When novices begin learning a skill, the coach gives them a rubric that describes the criteria for each stage of skill development. The novices use this rubric to determine their performance level of development. By comparing their performance with the clearly stated criteria, they decide what they are doing well and what steps they can take to improve. They also use the rubric to decide what help they want from the coach.

As they continue to practice and improve, the learners chart their way through the performance levels. By comparing their execution with the indicators in the performance rubric, the learners will continually change their self-evaluation. They will decide when they have moved from novice performer to advanced beginner, from advanced beginner to competent user, and so on.

At the same time that the learners are using the rubric to self-evaluate, the teacher or the learners' peers will observe their work and use the rubric to evaluate the learners' performance level. The teacher, peers, and learners will use frequent conferences to compare their evaluations of the learners' performance, discuss any differences in their evaluations, and identify goals for improvement. The learners will develop a plan for improving their performance and will ask the teacher or their peers for help in carrying out this plan. The learners may, for example, ask for more frequent feedback about what they are doing well and what they can do to improve their performance. This self, peer, and teacher evaluation process works well so long as everyone involved in the process maintains a dual focus: What are the learners doing well already, and what might they want to improve? The final evaluation of the performance learning task does not mean that the learners cannot continue to improve their skills. Growth and improvement stop only when developing the skill is no longer a high priority for the learners.

Novices

The coach introduces the novice musicians to their instruments and to sheet music. The coach helps the novices prepare for playing the instrument by demonstrating fingering, holding the instrument, and reading music. After the novices have had a chance to practice the latter, the coach and the novices read a fairly short piece of music together by having the novices hum the notes. At this point, the novices want to learn how to keep the notes flowing at a reasonable pace. Next, the novices practice using their instruments to play the notes, and coach and novices have another trial run. At the end of the novices' second test run, the coach and the learners assess progress. They discuss what the novices have learned, how to practice effective skill use, and how to adjust the performance for improvement.

Advanced Beginners

Once novices can coordinate music reading and fingering, they begin to practice playing music pieces in a way that maintains their rhythms. They focus more on the experience of making music than on the individual segments of the performance, although their primary focus is still on the performance. They still attend carefully to the coordination of fingering and notes on the page, but their music begins to flow. They can enjoy themselves during practice. Their mistakes become less frequent, and they begin to notice the emotion in the music. They and their coach discuss their learning and adjust their performance to further their skill development.

Competent Users

Competent musicians begin to think about the entire context of making music. They may begin to explore new and more challenging pieces. These musicians can now focus on the shifting moods and emotions and rhythms of the music. They may want to experiment with different tempos and volumes. As their skill progresses, they and their coach celebrate their success and look for more adjustments that will further develop their performance. Figure 1.1 shows a performance rubric for students who are learning music video design.

Proficient Performers

When proficient musicians are playing their instruments, they may realize that they are not thinking about the skill all of the time. They are enjoying the sound and feeling and are performing their music without conscious attention. As their playing becomes more and more automatic, they may find that they are now coaching novices. They are still very aware, when asked, of what they are doing and how it is working, and this awareness can help them become effective mentors to newcomers, because they can explain what to do and demonstrate how to do it without forgetting any of the elements that a beginner needs to know. Proficient performers often enjoy creating music. They are relaxed, happy, and confident when playing even difficult pieces.

Experts

Other musicians hear the expert play and say, "He's a natural." Experts are often so unaware of what they are doing that they cannot explain it to someone else. Their unconscious, effortless use of their skills ensures flawless performance. Because experts may forget about, or lose awareness of, key steps in skill development, they may not be effective as coaches. Their explanation or demonstration of a skill may omit details that novices need to be aware of in order to improve. Experts could be concert soloists with a major orchestra. Their performance abilities are so deeply embedded that they cannot imagine not knowing how to do the performance unconsciously and flawlessly.

Sometimes, novices do not have a clear picture of an expert performing the skill that the novices are learning. The coach and the novices can study models of excellence and use the rubric to assess the expert performance. A novice musician, for example, may watch video clips of artists in concert to see how experts make beautiful

Performance Rubric: Learning Brains and Music Strains

Developmental Level / Performance	Novice	Advanced Beginner	Competent User	Proficient Performer	Expert
Choreograph and Write Lyrics	Nothing matches! Does not synchronize words, music, and movements. Uses jerky movements and less than 50 percent of space. Speaks with inaudible voice. Mumbles and stumbles.	Fits words and movements to music 50 percent of time. Uses jerky movements and 75 percent of space. Speaks with audible voice. Speaks incomprehensibly.	Fits words and movements to music at least 80 percent of time. Uses smooth movements and 75 percent or more of space. Uses audible voice and understandable diction.	Synchronizes words, movements, and music. Moves smoothly, filling almost all of the space. Uses clear diction, good volume, and expression.	Composer's sister wrote the lyrics! Uses movements that are a natural fit! These kids belong in the Bolshoi Ballet company! Packs lyrics with expression and meaning!
Know the Composer	Gives correct name and close dates. Describes music vaguely. Provides no sponsor information. Provides no information on early influences. This could be any one of a dozen composers!	Gives correct name, dates, and family information. Omits composer's sponsor. Omits early influences. Gives one or two tidbits about composer's style.	Gives correct name, dates, and family and friend information. Names sponsor; provides no details of relationship. Cites one or two early influences. Describes style effectively.	Gives name, dates, family, friends, and details well. Tells good story of relationship with sponsor. Identifies and details early influences. Describes style and importance to composer's period well.	Provides wonderfully complete and accurate information. Writes thumbnail sketch of composer's life and loves that could be included in a published collection. Bravo!
Make Costumes and Set	Performs in school clothes in someone's bedroom! Wears regular clothes, not costumes. Works in insufficient space for moves.	Attempts to disguise clothes. Uses period-looking shirts. Uses some makeup (e.g., hair powder). Films in school cafeteria. Does not give attention to backgrounds. Works in adequate space.	Uses period shirts, knee pants. Uses hair powder and feather quill pens. Films in school auditorium in front of stage curtain; uses neutral background. Works in adequate space.	Uses period shirts, knee pants, brocade vests. Uses hair powder, quill pens. Creates parchment roll music. Performs on stage using backdrop curtain. Works in generous space.	Uses period shirts, knee pants, brocade vests; loafers with buckles. Uses hair powder and quill pens. Creates parchment roll music. Works in generous space.

Figure 1.1

Produce Biography	Provides no cover. Creates no illustrations. Leaves four or more typos in work. Uses unclear focus. Omits chronology. Does not use musical terms to describe composer's work.	Uses paper cover. Uses one or two illustrations. Leaves two or three typos in work. Provides most details in chronological order; adds one or two at the end. Focuses on composer. Describes work using musical terms.	Provides cardboard cover. Creates three or four illustrations including cover. Leaves only one typo in work. Focuses on composer and sponsor. Lists all life details in order. Describes music precisely.	Provides hard, illustrated cover. Creates four or five illustrations. Leaves no errors; uses clean copy. Focuses on composer, sponsor, and colleagues. Provides good chronology and use of musical terms. Nice job!	Uses hard, illustrated cover. Illustrates every page. Uses copy-quality printing. Tells engaging, interesting story. Awesome!
Create the Poster	Small, 18 by 24 inches. Leaves many smudges and finger marks. Leaves evidence of lots of corrections. Writes in small, faint letters. Includes small, colorless pictures.	24 by 24 inches. Leaves 2 or 3 smudges. Colors over white-out corrections. Writes large, but faint (or small and dark). Includes large illustrations, arranged poorly.	24 by 36 inches. Leaves no smudges or evidence of corrections. Writes legibly with large and dark characters. Includes large, interesting, colored illustrations, arranged well.	24 by 36 inches or larger. Very neat. Writes boldly and dramatically. Includes illustrations with good elements of composition and perspective.	24 by 36 inches or larger. Includes crisp illustrations. Writes dramatically and with emotional hook. Uses good composition, line, and perspective.

Figure 1.1

music. If an expert demonstrates signs of physical exhaustion at the end of a performance, the coach may comment that performing at that level is as tiring as running a marathon. The coach may also want to remind the novices that getting to the expert level takes years of practice and improvement and emphasize that the novices will go through all of the developmental stages on the road to becoming an excellent performer. Figure 1.2 shows the different focuses of the coach and the learners.

A chart for recording descriptions of performance levels for a classroom activity is included in the reproducibles at the end of this book.

WHY DOES PERFORMANCE LEARNING WORK?

Performance learning is brain-friendly learning that creates a positive emotional climate that enhances students' ability to remember ideas and concepts as the students perform tasks and learn skills. In this climate, students can reach a state of flow (Csikszentmihalyi, 1990). They feel pleasantly challenged, the novelty of the skill or task engages their interest, they can use the performance rubric to set personal goals and measure their progress, and they enjoy the learning experience. Teachers provide explicit instruction in the skills needed for the performance or task and also provide time for guided practice.

Students are asked to reflect on their performances, use a performance rubric to assess what they are doing well, and identify adjustments that could lead to improved performance. To round out the self-evaluation, students are asked to explain what help they need in improving their performances and what ideas, concepts, and skills they have learned. As they continually assess their performances, students learn lifelong self-evaluation and self-adjustment techniques that can help them lead happier, more satisfying lives.

Students who are performance learners develop intelligent behaviors (Costa, 2001) that can help them lead more effective lives: They become more flexible, more persistent, and more creative thinkers and doers who believe that they can learn and perform at a consistently high level of development.

Performance Development

Coach's Job

Give the learner models of expert performance.

Give the learner a rubric or performance checklist that outlines performance development stages.

Help the learner evaluate his or her performance.

Using the rubric, help the learner improve his or her performance.

Learner's Job

Use the rubric to evaluate present performance and identify what he or she can do.

Use the rubric to plan improvement in performance.

Ask the coach for help when needed.

Identify quality performance; maintain a vision of excellence.

Figure 1.2

PART I

Basic Performances

2

Rotting Peels and Cores

THE AUDIENCE

Grade Level

Students of all ages can learn how to turn garbage into compost. Teachers can find resources to use in urban or rural settings, indoors or out of doors, with learners from kindergarten through high school. Teachers can find a wealth of information about designing composting units by using an Internet search engine such as Google or Dogpile to search for "composting in school" and similar phrases.

Diverse Learners

Careful assigning of students to cooperative learning teams can result in maximum learning for all. See the Preface for suggestions about team roles and responsibilities. For this performance learning activity, the Correspondent will keep the team field notebook and prepare the presentation bar and pie charts; the Conductor will perform the measurements and produce required sketches; and the Dry Cell will mix the developing compost, add water or dirt as needed, and produce the final draft of the pamphlet. All team members will help in assembling the compost materials, managing the compost pile, and preparing and editing the rough draft of the pamphlet. By carefully matching each student to a role, the teacher encourages feelings of relaxed alertness that lead to deeper learning (Caine et al., 2005).

Before teachers introduce this activity to students, they will look over the task development chart and the performance rubric to decide which tasks are appropriate for their grade level or for individual students. Each student will, for example, keep an individual field notebook, and the performance level targets and ways of recording information for individual students will be different. Teachers will also need to adapt the activity for the developmental level of their students.

THE PERFORMANCE

As populations increase and available space for waste disposal decreases, more and more communities are adopting waste reduction policies and requirements. In some communities, each household still receives unlimited waste pickup service. In other communities, each household is limited to a maximum amount of waste that will be collected per pickup. Waste collection agencies are encouraging people to "reduce, reuse, and recycle" as much as possible.

One effective technique for reducing food scrap (and yard) waste is composting. As students learn to manage a compost pile so that these wastes are converted to rich fertilizer, they learn important science and social studies ideas and concepts and practice key math and language arts skills. As students assemble and manage compost piles, they will keep careful records of the techniques they use, how well those procedures work, how much time is needed to produce the compost, and how the final product can be used. Students will keep samples of the compost produced in several trials and display these during the final exhibition of learning.

Students will learn that they can construct and manage their compost piles in relatively small indoor spaces. Resources are available to guide both urban and rural students as they learn composting techniques. At this time, the Web site http://journey toforever.org/compost.html includes a list of books and Web sites that include ideas for composting in elementary, middle school, and high school classrooms.

To prepare for the final demonstration of learning, students will learn how to effectively communicate their composting research and its results. Some tools that they will use are oral descriptions of their composting processes and procedures, charts and graphs illustrating the processes, a brochure explaining composting, and a discussion of community attitudes toward waste disposal. Students will use these tools as they present their composting research results to their classmates or other audiences.

The Prompt

Several natural or organic fertilizing products available in gardening shops are composts. Mushroom compost is one of the richest products available.

The teacher introduces students to this performance task by displaying several such products and then asking, "Do you know what compost is? Can you tell me where this comes from? Is it made in a factory? The label says 'organic.' What does that mean? Could you make this at home? What might you need to know?" Answers to these questions will show that compost is the end product of food scraps and yard waste. The product can be made at home, and students and their parents can manage a compost pile effectively by applying principles that affect the speed of physical or chemical changes. This activity will help students learn the composting techniques that will result in successful home composting.

The teacher will tell students that when they present the results of their learning to an audience, they need to be able to describe the different composting procedures they tried, identify the techniques that produced the best compost in a specific amount of time, display the final compost samples and the notebooks containing their records, exhibit charts and graphs comparing composting conditions and results, and give each member of the audience a brochure about composting. When the teacher introduces this task to the students, he or she will also announce the exhibition date.

The Vision

Examples of excellent composting results and presentations of learning will give students a clear picture of the teacher's expectations. If this is a performance learning task teachers have used in previous years, they will show samples of high-quality compost prepared by former students. Compost samples will keep well from year to year if teachers seal them tightly in plastic bags.

Students also will view videos of excellent presentations that demonstrate clear, concise, dynamic communication of the composting research and conclusions. The teacher will obtain videotapes of televised gardening programs that portray demonstrations of effective composting. Students and teachers can analyze commercial posters for visual effectiveness and can discuss the elements they expect in an excellent expository presentation. As part of their commitment to excellence in local schools, nurseries and gardening shops will be encouraged to donate copies of commercial brochures explaining the uses of compost for students to inspect.

Before students begin the performance task, the teacher will want to be sure that they are familiar with the elements of effective field studies and excellent exhibitions of learning. To be effective learners, students must begin with the end in mind (Covey, 1989).

The Standards

As the composting begins, students need to know what tasks they need to do to reach their goal. The teacher can show them an overview of the performance tasks, the developmental levels of the performance, and the content ideas and concepts they will be learning by using a task development chart (see Figure 2.1).

From the day they begin the performance task, students are preparing for the final exhibition of learning. To help them prepare a quality performance, teachers will provide a performance rubric (see Figure 2.2) when they assign the performance task. Students can use the performance rubric to self-evaluate their progress. They can see how their performance or products compare with the descriptions in the rubric, adjust and improve their work, and work toward a quality exhibition of learning. Every piece of the final performance that will be evaluated is listed in this rubric. Using the rubric will allow the teacher and each student to differentiate the curriculum by tailoring the activity to the child's level of readiness (Tomlinson, 1999).

THE COACHING CONTEXT

Setting Up the Task

After presenting the prompt and the vision, the teacher will outline the performance task for the students. The composting task will be done by teams composed of three students whose roles and responsibilities are outlined in *The Audience* section of this chapter. The teacher will assign the students to teams and give the teams time to get organized. Then the teacher will outline the requirements for the final presentation and will explain that each team will need to experiment with at least four different compost piles to examine the importance of scrap size, moisture, added ingredients, and mixing on the speed with which the garbage turns into compost.

For very young students, the teacher explains that they will need to have one compost pile that is their "control," a pile for which the scrap size and the other variables are predetermined. The teacher suggests that this control compost pile contain small food scraps (bigger scraps may be cut or torn to get the desired size) that are kept slightly moist at all times. The teacher tells students to add a little dirt and possibly a few worms at the beginning of the process and to mix or stir this compost pile every two or three days. The goal is to have high-quality compost by the announced exhibition date.

The teacher suggests that the second compost pile contain large scraps that are kept moist, have dirt and worms added, and be stirred every two or three days; that the third pile contain small scraps that are kept dry, have dirt and worms added, and be stirred every two or three days; and that the last pile contain small scraps that are kept moist, have no added dirt or worms, and be stirred as the others are. Students will do an additional compost pile that is not stirred at all to investigate the importance of mixing. To keep the investigation manageable, the teacher tells students that they will be using small-scale compost piles.

Students will put three or four cups of food scraps in a plastic milk bottle to start each compost pile. The teacher will ask each student to bring in a one-gallon, high-density polyurethane recyclable container, such as the type used for milk and distilled water. Then, the teacher or the students can cut off the top one-third, including the handle, of each container using a scissors. This plastic is soft enough to cut quite easily, and the resulting container will hold the composting mixture without leaking. If students bring in the caps for the plastic containers, the cut-off portions may be used to loosely cover the compost piles and reduce odors in the classroom. To label their compost piles, students can write on the plastic with permanent markers.

The teacher will ask each student to bring in a plastic container a few weeks before the class is to start the task, so that the compost containers are available at the beginning of the performance learning task. When students begin working with composting processes, the teacher will ask each of them to bring in a bag of food scraps from home to use in their compost piles. Each student will contribute five or six cups of food scraps to the team supply and will bring the scraps to class on the day that the composting process starts.

To protect the health and safety of the students, the teacher will require that they wear rubber gloves when they work with compost and wash their hands thoroughly before handling any food or touching their faces.

Keeping the Notebook

The teacher will explain to the students that each person needs to keep a field notebook that is a complete record of the compost pile: its set-up, how often it is watered and mixed, any other actions used with the compost, and how the appearance and odor of the mixture changes each time the team works with the compost. A complete record will include sketches and photos of the compost piles at various times during the trial. To help students organize their records, the teacher suggests a format for the field notebook entries (see Figure. 2.3).

Timelines

Even the best-managed compost pile needs time to convert raw food scraps into finished product. At the beginning of the task, the teacher will tell the students that

(Text continued on page 18)

Task Development Chart: Rotting Peels and Cores

Performance Tasks	Developmental Levels	Curriculum Standards
Set up and manage the compost pile. Collect appropriate raw material. Manage scrap size, moisture, and additional ingredients effectively. Mix as needed for best results.	**Novice** Scraps rot very little. Notebook contains initial entry and little else. Graphs are small, unlabeled, and messy. Pamphlet contains at least five factual or mechanical errors. Presentation is stilted and inaudible.	**Science** Collect and interpret data. Identify and describe physical and chemical changes. Analyze factors affecting the speed of a change. Discuss food web principles. Demonstrate basic safety practices.
Keep a detailed field notebook that includes a record of everything done to each compost pile and the results. These records include measurements, descriptions, and sketches or photos of the compost piles over time.	**Advanced Beginner** 30 percent of scraps rot. Notebook contains initial and final entries and little else. Graphs are small, unclearly labeled, and messy. Pamphlet contains four factual or mechanical errors. Presentation is stilted, but audible.	**Math** Display results in bar and pie graphs. Weigh raw materials accurately. Calculate percentages: weight of compost to weight of raw material.
Produce a bar graph comparing rotting times in the different compost piles. Prepare a pie graph showing the percent of the original material that rotted into compost in the different compost piles.	**Competent User** 60 percent of scraps rot. Notebook contains initial and final entries and a few others. Graphs are small, clearly labeled, and clean. Pamphlet contains three factual or mechanical errors. Presentation is rehearsed, smooth, and audible.	**Social Studies** Analyze effect of human activity on land. Describe attitudes toward land use. Identify individual contributions to social problems.
Prepare a pamphlet explaining how composting creates a useful product while reducing solid waste. Include a resources list in the pamphlet.	**Proficient Performer** 80 percent of scraps rot. Notebook contains entries for most compost work. Graphs are large, clearly labeled, and clean. Pamphlet contains one or two factual or mechanical errors. Presentation is relaxed, rehearsed, and entertaining.	**Language Arts** Write persuasively. Demonstrate subject/verb agreement. Edit for spelling and capitalization.
Present the results of the composting trials. Use teamwork and visual aids to enhance the presentation.	**Expert** Almost 100 percent of scraps rot. Notebook contains illustrated entries for all compost work. Graphs are large, clearly labeled, and clean. Pamphlet contains no factual or mechanical errors. Presentation is relaxed, rehearsed, and entertaining.	**Library Media and Technology** Find information on the Internet. Build a resources list that includes books, magazines, journals, and Web sites.

Figure 2.1

Performance Rubric: Rotting Peels and Cores

Developmental Level / Performance	Novice	Advanced Beginner	Competent User	Proficient Performer	Expert
Make Compost	Large, unchanged food scraps. Little, if any, rotting. Really bad smell (forgotten leftovers).	Some small pieces of unchanged food. Crumbling and rotting around the edges. "Dirt and worms" smell.	Small, light colored chunks. "What was this?" Soft and crumbly.	Small dark chunks. Some of compost is like crumbly dirt. Unique smell (may be quite strong).	Dark, crumbly, small pieces. Looks and acts like topsoil. Unique smell (may really stink!).
Keep a Field Notebook	Sketchy notes. No clear record of what was done when. No clear notes on results.	Clearly dated entries. Some missing information about scrap size, moisture, mixing, and additions. Little information about results.	Clearly dated entries. Charts showing scrap size, moisture, mixing, and additions are complete and clear. Some information on results.	Dates and times for all entries. Charts and descriptions of work done. Some sketches. Information on most results.	Dates and weather conditions for all entries. Charts, descriptions of work done. Sketches of compost piles and tools. Complete results; includes photos.
Create Bar and Pie Graph Posters	Small (10 by 20 cm or smaller). Faint, blurry, black and white, smudgy. Small images and writing. Confusing labels.	Small (20 by 20 cm). Black and white, legible at three meters. Some smudges or blurs. Clear labels.	Medium (50 by 50 cm). Some light color. Clean and unsmudged. Legible at three meters. Clear labels and legends.	Large (50 by 100 cm). Some bright colors. Clean, unsmudged. Legible at five meters. Clear labels and legends.	Large (50 by 100 cm). Bold, primary colors. Black outlines, crisp edges. Legible beyond five meters. Needs no explaining!

Figure 2.2

Write a Persuasive Pamphlet	Unclear message. Four or more errors in spelling, capitalization, or subject/verb agreement. At least three sentence fragments.	Message can be understood on second or third reading. Four errors in spelling, capitalization, or subject/verb agreement. One or two sentence fragments.	Message is clear but not supported. Three errors in spelling, capitalization, or subject/verb agreement. No sentence fragments.	Message is clear with one or two supporting pieces. One or two errors in spelling, capitalization, or subject/verb agreement. No sentence fragments.	Message is clear with three or more supporting pieces. No errors in spelling, capitalization, or subject/verb agreement. No sentence fragments. It convinces me!
Participate in the Oral Presentation	Mutters and mumbles. Whispery voice. Solo speaker for team. Little or no eye contact.	Very low voices. Words clearly pronounced (if audience is close enough to hear). Two speakers for the team, who glance at the audience.	Can be heard at a distance of five meters. Clear pronunciation and some inflection. All team members speak and look at the audience.	Audible at seven meters. Clear pronunciation and "feeling" inflections. Team members take turns speaking. Solid eye contact.	Loud, clear, and spoken with feeling. Relaxed speakers engage the audience. Bravo! Bravo!

Figure 2.2

Date:

Weather conditions:

Compost pile number:

What we did to this compost pile today:

Appearance of this compost pile today:

Food scraps we can still identify:

Sketches:

Figure 2.3

(Text continued from page 14)

they will work with their compost piles for six weeks. During this time, students also will be planning their final performances, keeping their field notebooks, and planning their pamphlets and graph posters. Two weeks after completing their work with the compost piles, students will do the presentation performances. During those two weeks, the teacher will work with teams to help them assess their presentations, adjust and correct, and prepare quality materials for the final exhibition.

The Graph Posters

Each team will prepare two graph posters to show the effectiveness of the different composting techniques. One poster will show a bar graph and the other a pie graph.

For the bar graph, students will draw a vertical bar showing the days needed for half of the scraps in a pile to become black, crumbly compost. Figure 2.4 shows the time for scraps to become compost for two compost piles as indicated by the bars. Students indicate that the bars are for different compost piles by using different colors or patterns for the bars. The title of the graph says that students are discovering how to change the speed of a physical or chemical change.

As students set up their compost piles, they weigh the food scraps they are using. At the end of six weeks, the students will sort out any large pieces of remaining food scraps and weigh them. Teams can use these data to calculate the percent of the food scraps in each pile that rotted into compost. They will use pie graphs to show this information. Figure 2.5 shows pie graphs for two compost piles.

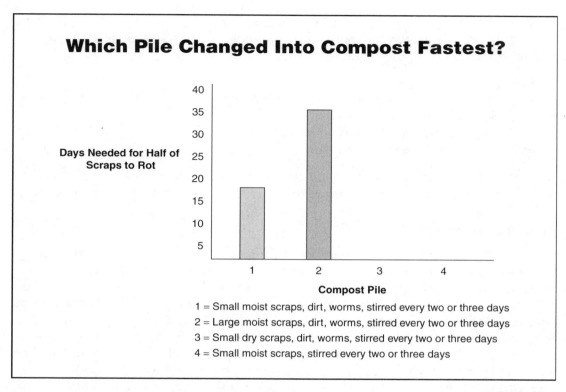

Figure 2.4

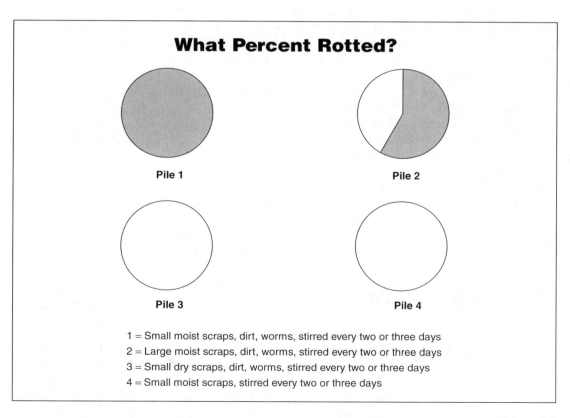

Figure 2.5

The teacher will provide the rubric criteria. Then, the teacher and the students will brainstorm the rubric indicators. For example, they could decide that effective graph posters have the following elements:

- Large size (at least 50 by 100 cm)
- Bold colors (bright, primary colors or blends)
- Dark, clear lettering
- Legibility from a distance of at least five meters
- Labels, legends, and title explaining the graphs

The performance exhibition rubric also contains criteria for the posters. Student teams will use the rubric to identify requirements for high-quality graph posters.

The Persuasive Pamphlet

As part of the final performance, each student team will prepare a pamphlet in which they highlight the advantages of composting instead of sending food scraps to the landfill. Many communities have information available about the decreasing availability of landfill space, and the teacher will obtain a supply of brochures with this information for the students. The teacher will also ask students to get information about composting, recycling (since composting actually recycles nutrients), and food webs from the local or school library or the Internet. The teacher will tell students that they will be creating a resources list for people who want more information about composting. Students can find Web sites by using a search engine to find information about "composting," "compost piles," or "creating compost."

Students will demonstrate their editing skills as they check their writing for subject/verb agreement, correct spelling, and correct capitalization. Students and teacher will brainstorm the performance indicators for the persuasive pamphlet, and they will brainstorm a detailed checklist of pamphlet features. Possible features include the following:

- Has a catchy title
- Presents a positive argument
- Focuses on solutions, not problems
- Contains relevant information
- Is brief
- Has a message
- Looks good

Students will use the performance rubric and the checklist to assess and improve their pamphlets until they are convinced they are presentation quality.

THE PRESENTATION

When the teacher introduces this performance learning task to the students, he or she will tell them about the final presentation they will make to their classmates or a wider audience. Because everyone in the class is involved in a similar performance task, the teacher and class may decide they want to demonstrate their learning to an outside audience, such as another class in the school. The teacher can make these arrangements.

The students and teacher will review the elements to be included in the oral presentation. Students will want to inform their audience about the task's background—their

Rotting Peels and Cores Differences

Factor \ Pile	1	2	3	4
Scrap Size	Small	Large	Small	Small
Moist or Dry	Moist	Moist	Dry	Moist
Additions	Dirt, worms	Dirt, worms	Dirt, worms	—
Mixing	Every two or three days	Every two or three days	Every two or three days	Every two or three days

Figure 2.6

reasons for learning about composting. These reasons could include the social studies and science standards students are working toward as they do this task. Students will tell the audience what they did. They will describe the experiment's design and their composting results. To illustrate their performances, students will use their graph posters and may decide to prepare other visual aids. They may, for example, decide to produce a poster showing how scrap size, moisture level, added ingredients, and mixing varied among compost piles (see Figure 2.6).

Each team will prepare a copy of its persuasive pamphlet for each member of the target audience, and team members will distribute these pamphlets during the presentation. If funding for producing a large number of pamphlets is a problem, the teacher can investigate the possibility of obtaining a minigrant or ask for help from the PTO or a community service organization. The team will have sealed bags of the compost from each pile available for members of the audience to inspect.

The teacher will show videos of news presentations and ask students to analyze what makes these presentations effective. To illustrate the difference between more and less engaging presentations, the teacher will want to include several clips, some that are very engaging (e.g., a reporter broadcasting from a toy show or during a storm) and others that are less involving (e.g., "talking heads").

Students will be given time to practice and polish their presentations during class. The teacher will make video equipment available so students can actually see and hear their performances during rehearsals, compare them with the performance rubric, and polish them into high-quality, engaging exhibitions of learning.

THE REFLECTION

Each group will do a PMI chart (de Bono, 1976) to reflect on and process its actions and learning. Group members will discuss the pluses, minuses, and interesting features of doing composting as a performance task. A PMI chart is included in the reproducibles at the end of this book.

Each student will complete several sentence starters as an individual reflection and meet with teammates to share responses. The team and individual reflections will help students cement their learning and form better cognitive patterns. Reflection also increases student awareness of the learning process and helps students expand their repertoires of effective learning tools.

Reflection

TEAM REFLECTION
Doing a Compost Pile

Pluses (+'s)
Minuses (−'s)
Interesting (!?'s)

INDIVIDUAL REFLECTION
What I'm Thinking

- Three science learnings that I got from this task are _____

- My favorite science learning is _____ because _____

- Two writing skills I improved are _____

- I know these skills improved because _____

- One idea I'll remember about how I can help my community is _____

- This idea is important because _____

- Here's how my science learning can help me do these food preparations faster: dissolve gelatin, cook vegetables _____

_____

_____

3

Learning Brains and Music Strains

THE AUDIENCE

Grade Level

This performance learning activity works well for students from Grade 3 through high school. Ross (2006) reports that programs designed to introduce inner-city children to classical music receive strong support from students and their parents, while Prescott (2005) reports that students in isolated, rural communities embrace music education that links classroom experiences to everyday life. Teachers can find information about outreach programs offered by the St. Paul Chamber Orchestra to urban schools at http://www.thespco.org. Students from all socioeconomic backgrounds and communities can connect with and find meaning in classical music.

Diverse Learners

Careful assigning of students to cooperative learning teams can result in maximum learning for all. See the Preface for suggestions about team roles and responsibilities. For this performance learning activity, the Conductor will lead group production of the booklet, a Correspondent/Poet will select music from a classical or baroque composer for use in a music video and polish the team-generated lyrics for the video, and the Dry Cell/Choreographer will plan the movements that synchronize with the music and lyrics. By carefully matching each student to a role, the teacher encourages feelings of relaxed alertness that lead to deeper learning (Caine et al., 2005).

Before teachers introduce this activity to students, they will look over the task development chart and the performance rubric to decide which tasks are appropriate for their grade level or for individual students. Using the rubric will allow the teacher and each student to differentiate the curriculum by tailoring the activity to the child's level of readiness (Tomlinson, 1999). Teachers will also need to adapt the activity for the developmental level of their students.

THE PERFORMANCE

Musical and rhythmic intellectual capabilities develop in every person before birth. Lazear (2003) says that no other intellectual capacity develops earlier, and researchers suggest that learners who acquire information and ideas as they listen to certain kinds of music embed that information into their long-term memories. In examining why this is true, Jensen (1995) says that because music activates the limbic system along with the right brain, and because of the emotional component associated with music, the brain is more likely to form neural networks to encode this information in long-term memory. Teachers of young children traditionally use music to glue information in their students' minds. Many adults still "sing" the alphabet in their heads to remember the order of the letters. This is powerful testimony about the importance of music to learning.

Georgi Lozanov (1978) and other researchers have found that many kinds of music, including New Age, jazz, rock, folk, pop, and country as well as baroque and classical, can enhance learning. The music forms that produce the most predictable learning results are classical and baroque, especially adagios and largos, and partic-ularly pieces incorporating higher frequencies. Lozanov recommends that students listen to classical- or romantic-era music during new learning and to baroque music during review. Mozart is the composer whose work is most often associated with enhanced learning, and for this reason, the link between learning and music is some-times referred to as the Mozart effect.

Some of the best-known research on this connection came from Rauscher and her team (Rauscher, Shaw, & Ky, 1993) at the University of California, Irvine. Three groups of students participated in an experiment in which each student took an intelligence test after engaging in a specific focus activity prior to the test. The con-trol group sat in a quiet room for ten minutes, the second group listened to a relax-ation tape for ten minutes, and the third group listened to ten minutes of Mozart's *Sonata for Two Pianos in D Major.* All participants then took the Stanford-Binet IQ test. The Mozart group scored eight to nine points higher on the spatial portion than either of the other two groups.

In further studies, Dr. Rauscher and her team found that the increase in spatial IQ scores lasted for just a few days when students linked music to mental rehearsal for a single testing event. When students used music consistently during learning or review over several months (or years), the Irvine group found that the students experienced long-term increases in intellectual capabilities, particularly in spatial-temporal skills.

Other research suggests that strategic use of music can help students learn a new language faster and master basic skills in their first language (Prescott, 2005). Children who are experiencing difficulties with language particularly benefit from this practice. Jensen (2002) cites research supporting the view that music has strong positive neurological systemwide effects, possibly because music seems to be hardwired into our genes.

Many students may not be familiar with classical and baroque music. In this performance learning task, students will listen to selections by several classical and baroque composers and will work in teams of three to produce music videos featuring a work by one of the composers.

Students will use an instrumental recording of the composer's work to accompany their performance of lyrics and actions. The lyrics will highlight key information about the composer and his work and associates, so teams will need to research the composer's life to learn about his development as a musician, important early influences on his music, his sponsors, contemporary reviews of his works, his general acceptance or rejection by his peers, and details of his personal life. To link classical composers to the students' everyday experiences, the teacher will ask questions such as, "Did his parents consider the composer to be a problem child? Where did your composer find his most enthusiastic audience? Do you hear any rhythms or musical phrases that link the composer's music to your favorite music? Why might this composer be considered the biggest rap (or rock) star of his day?"

Each student team will prepare an illustrated booklet—a companion piece to the music video—in which the team summarizes this information. For the presentation performance, student teams will create a poster that advertises their work, the music video, and the booklet. As teams do their presentations, they will relate the information from the booklet to their classmates, show the video, and answer questions about the composer and their insights into the role of music in learning.

The teacher will help students expand their understanding of the link between music and learning and will encourage students to listen to classical and baroque music at home. Students who want to purchase music can find many collections that contain brain-friendly movements from the works of these composers. The school music teacher or a clerk at a local music store can help students select pieces to play softly during learning and reflection. By learning about these composers and their music in this performance context, students are more likely to choose classical music as background music when faced with a challenging new learning task.

The Prompt

For several days before introducing this performance learning task to the students, the teacher will use classical or baroque background music in the ways suggested by Lozanov (1978). As students work on new learning in small groups, the teacher will play selections from classical composers at low volume. While students reflect on their learning or write in their journals, the teacher will play baroque selections. When students begin to question this use of music in the classroom, the teacher will introduce the performance task. At this time, the teacher will tell students about the research that supports this use of music and will emphasize that the music being used to enhance learning has the most predictable results.

The students and the teacher will brainstorm examples of times when the students have used music or rhythm to enhance new learning. Someone will probably mention the alphabet song. Another student may have learned a song that teaches the names of the planets in order of their distances from the sun. Many students will remember the names of Santa's reindeer from hearing "Rudolph the Red-Nosed Reindeer." As they brainstorm, students will become more aware of the power of music in learning.

The teacher will assign students to teams of three and will introduce and assign team roles. To outline the performance learning task and presentation, the teacher will explain that the whole class will listen to and discuss selections from works by several baroque and classical composers, that each individual will record information about the musical selections and his or her enjoyment of the pieces in a listening log, and that each team will select one composer and produce a music video featuring a piece from one of his or her works. Teams may rework the music to align it more closely with their everyday listening, and the song must be recognizable as the classical or baroque piece upon which it is based. The team will research the composer's musical and personal life and write lyrics that feature some of the information the team members learn to accompany their selected piece of music.

Teammates will practice presenting the song as they perform the movements planned by their choreographer. They may use the original rhythms and phrasings found in the classical piece, or they may jazz it up or "rap it up." The final presentation performance will feature the music video, the illustrated booklet that summarizes the composer's life and work, and the poster advertising the presentation.

The Vision

To produce performance-level music videos of their own, students need to be aware of the features of professional work. The teacher will show carefully selected music videos to the class and then lead a brainstorming session to analyze and list the attributes of an expert-level music video. Some elements that will appear on this list are appropriate vocal volume, clear diction, good fit of lyrics to musical rhythms, good coordination between lyrics and actions, effective costumes, appropriate backgrounds, and enthusiastic performance of the piece of music.

The teacher also will provide carefully selected examples of movie posters for students to analyze. The teacher will ask, "What features of these posters get you interested in moving closer to read the fine print? Do you want to see these movies? Why? What do these posters do to hook your interest?" The students and teacher will brainstorm a list of successful poster features, such as effective colors, large illustrations, clear lettering, use of action words, and emotional references (e.g., Audiences love it! The creature you'll love to hate!). Movie theaters often are happy to donate old posters to schools, so the teacher will be able to obtain these professional examples.

The Standards

Students who have no experience in matching lyrics to melody will need reassurance that songwriting takes time. The teacher will want to mention sources of help for beginning lyricists, such as rhyming dictionaries and thesauruses. Searching for "rhyming dictionary" online gives students and teacher many resources from which they can choose. The teacher will encourage students to work on lyrics in their teams, because team brainstorming often unleashes creativity. The team poet will refine and polish these lyrics and submit the edited version to the team for final approval.

Early in the performance learning task, the teacher will give students the task development chart (see Figure 3.1), use it to explain and clarify the task, and answer questions the students have about the final performance. To help students understand the long-term goals of this performance task, the teacher will focus their attention on the listening behaviors described in the developmental levels column and say, "My long-term goal is to help you become more effective learners. I know that you can use this music as a tool to enhance and deepen your learning, and I hope that you choose to use baroque and classical music as a learning background at home and at school. As we learn about these periods in music history, you will be teaching each other about some of the composers and their work, and you will have information that you can use to select brain-friendly learning and review music." The teacher will also provide students with information about research linking use of music to enhanced learning.

When students do the final performance for this learning task, they will display and explain the poster, summarize and display the composer biography booklet, show the music video to the class, and answer questions about the composer's life and music. To help students prepare quality presentations, the teacher will give them the performance rubric (see Figure 3.2) as they begin the learning task.

THE COACHING CONTEXT

Background Music

As teachers begin to use background music, they inform the students they will be working with these pieces and others in the near future. Teachers tell their students that they want them to listen with open minds and learn to appreciate the music. Teachers instruct the students to keep a listening log in which they record information about their thinking about each piece of music.

The teacher will write the name of each music selection, the composer's name, and the music period (baroque or classical) on the chalkboard each day. Each student will give a quick "thumbs-up, thumbs-down" enjoyment rating to each piece and briefly explain the reason for each rating. Students will provide more detailed information about each selection in their listening logs (see Figure 3.3).

Music Exploration

Before student teams select their composers and gather biographical information, the teacher and students will take some time to listen to and analyze music together. The teacher will help students determine meter and pacing by explaining the music terms for pacing and playing examples so students can hear pacing differences. The students and teacher will discuss the emotional feelings they experience while listening to these music selections. To show students how to strengthen their explanations with references to the music, the teacher will provide some examples such as, "When I listen to the first few minutes of Vivaldi's 'Spring,' I feel very happy. The up-tempo pacing and higher-frequency notes give me a feeling of energy. I want to dance to this music. The trilling sounds to me like birds singing in the spring. I really like spring. I enjoy seeing the new growth and smelling the fresh air."

Because some students may feel self-conscious about describing their reflections and feelings about the music for the whole class, students will begin these discussions in their small, video-production teams. The important point is to help students realize that music helps cement learning by engaging the emotions, and the teacher will want students to discuss and analyze their involvement with

(Text continued on page 31)

Task Development Chart: Learning Brains and Music Strains

Performance Tasks	Developmental Levels	Curriculum Standards
Novice Listen to and keep a log of background music. Be aware of emotions elicited by the music (e.g., sad, happy, calm, excited) and develop a feel for classical and baroque music.	**Novice** Strongly dislikes classical and baroque music. Says, "This stuff is dumb! I want my MTV!" Asks, "Mozart who? Which Bach? What's a Vivaldi?" Doesn't recognize or identify emotional component of listening to music.	**Performing Arts** Identify and effectively combine choreography elements; use movement expressively. Identify musical elements such as rhythm, melody, and form (e.g., rondo, theme, variation). Identify music pacing (e.g., allegretto, andante, adagio). Synchronize movement with music.
Advanced Beginner Meet the music video team and decide on roles. Pick the music piece for the video. Brainstorm the lyrics. Create lyrics for four to five minutes of music. Research background information on composer and musical period. Create rough drafts: booklet, advertising poster.	**Advanced Beginner** Listens to classical and baroque without complaining. Recognizes some names: Haydn, Bach, Handel. Leisure listening does not include classical or baroque music. Recognizes emotions elicited by music. Explains the importance of music sponsors.	**Visual Arts** Produce graphics that demonstrate effective composition and use of color, line, and perspective.
Competent User Rehearse polished lyrics with music. Rehearse synchronized choreography. Plan costumes and pick a set. Revise booklet and poster; produce the presentation copies. Help with timeline showing composers and dates.	**Competent User** Enjoys classical and baroque selections played in class. Recognizes some pieces and names the composers. Feels strong emotions when listening to some pieces. Might change leisure listening habits: "Maybe someday. This stuff really isn't so bad." Will go to live performances if someone else pays.	**Mathematics** Analyze music timing and express results as a ratio. Produce a marked-to-scale timeline that includes the composers featured in all of the class's music video productions.
Proficient Performer Complete costumes and set. Make the video. Sing or chant the lyrics. Keep lyrics synchronized with music. Perform the choreographed movements smoothly.	**Proficient Performer** Taps foot, keeps time with hand, smiles when listening to classical or baroque music. Leisure listening occasionally includes classical or baroque selections. Knows personal history of favorite composers. Will buy own ticket for live performance.	**Language Arts** Produce writing that shows sharp focus, precise use of language, logical organization of ideas, and appropriate support of main points. Demonstrate clear understanding of composer's biographical information.
Expert Do presentation performance: Introduce composer using the poster and booklet. Show the video. Answer questions about the composer. Display poster and booklet. Be ready to loan video to classmates.	**Expert** Enjoys listening to classical or baroque music and shows it through body language. Owns several classical or baroque compact discs. Listens to classical or baroque music several times a week. Sponsors local music organization or public radio. Has a season ticket to symphony or opera.	**Library Media and Technology** Find musical period and composer information using the Internet. Evaluate the usefulness and accuracy of sources of information.

Figure 3.1

Performance Rubric: Learning Brains and Music Strains

Developmental Level / Performance	Novice	Advanced Beginner	Competent User	Proficient Performer	Expert
Choreograph and Write Lyrics	Nothing matches! Does not synchronize words, music, and movements. Uses jerky movements and less than 50 percent of space. Speaks with inaudible voice. Mumbles and stumbles.	Fits words and movements to music 50 percent of time. Uses jerky movements and 75 percent of space. Speaks with audible voice. Speaks incomprehensibly.	Fits words and movements to music at least 80 percent of time. Uses smooth movements and 75 percent or more of space. Uses audible voice and understandable diction.	Synchronizes words, movements, and music. Moves smoothly, filling almost all of the space. Uses clear diction, good volume, and expression.	Composer's sister wrote the lyrics! Uses movements that are a natural fit! These kids belong in the Bolshoi Ballet company! Packs lyrics with expression and meaning!
Know the Composer	Gives correct name and close dates. Describes music vaguely. Provides no sponsor information. Provides no information on early influences. This could be any one of a dozen composers!	Gives correct name, dates, and family information. Omits composer's sponsor. Omits early influences. Gives 1 or 2 tidbits about composer's style.	Gives correct name, dates, family, and friend information. Names sponsor; provides no details of relationship. Cites 1 or 2 early influences. Describes style effectively.	Gives name, dates, family, friends, and details well. Tells good story of relationship with sponsor. Identifies and details early influences. Describes style and importance to composer's period well.	Provides wonderfully complete and accurate information. Writes thumbnail sketch of composer's life and loves that could be included in a published collection. Bravo!
Make Costumes and Set	Performs in school clothes in someone's bedroom! Wears regular clothes, not costumes. Works in insufficient space for moves.	Attempts to disguise clothes. Uses period-looking shirts. Uses some makeup (e.g., hair powder). Films in school cafeteria. Does not give attention to backgrounds. Works in adequate space.	Uses period shirts, knee pants. Uses hair powder, feather quill pens. Films in school auditorium in front of stage curtain; uses neutral background. Works in adequate space.	Uses period shirts, knee pants, brocade vests. Uses hair powder, quill pens. Creates parchment roll music. Performs on stage using backdrop curtain. Works in generous space.	Uses period shirts, knee pants, brocade vests; loafers with buckles. Uses hair powder and quill pens. Creates parchment roll music. Works in generous space.

Figure 3.2 (*Continued*)

Performance Rubric: Learning Brains and Music Strains (Continued)

Developmental Level / Performance	Novice	Advanced Beginner	Competent User	Proficient Performer	Expert
Produce Biography	Provides no cover. Creates no illustrations. Leaves 4 or more typos. Uses unclear focus. Omits chronology. Does not use musical terms to describe composer's work.	Provides paper cover. Creates 1 or 2 illustrations. Leaves 2 or 3 typos. Provides most details in chronological order; adds 1 or 2 at the end. Focuses on composer. Describes work using musical terms.	Provides cardboard cover. Creates 3 or 4 illustrations including cover. Leaves only 1 typo. Focuses on composer and sponsor. Lists all life details in order. Describes music precisely.	Provides hard, illustrated cover. Creates 4 or 5 illustrations. Leaves no errors; uses clean copy. Focuses on composer, sponsor, colleagues. Provides good chronology and use of musical terms. Nice job!	Provides hard, illustrated cover. Illustrates every page. Uses copy-quality printing. Tells engaging, interesting story. Awesome!
Create the Poster	Small, 18 × 24 inches. Leaves many smudges and finger marks. Leaves evidence of lots of corrections. Writes in small, faint letters. Includes small, colorless pictures.	24 × 24 inches. Leaves 2 or 3 smudges. Colors over white-out corrections. Writes large, but faint (or small and dark). Includes large illustrations, arranged poorly.	24 × 36 inches. Leaves no smudges or evidence of corrections. Writes legibly with large and dark characters. Includes large, interesting, colored illustrations, arranged well.	24 × 36 inches or larger. Very neat. Writes boldly and dramatically. Uses illustrations with good elements of composition and perspective.	24 × 36 inches or larger. Includes crisp illustrations. Writes dramatically and with emotional hook. Uses good composition, line, and perspective.

Figure 3.2

Brain-Building Music Log

Date:

Name of Musical Selection:

Composer: Period: | Baroque | Classical |

Enjoyment Rating: Reason(s) for Rating:

| ↑ | ↓ | ←→ |

Figure 3.3

(Text continued from page 27)

the music in an emotionally safe setting that promotes higher-order thinking and deeper learning.

Researching the Composers

Students will need to gather some information about their composers and the music periods in which they worked. The teacher will remind them to find biographical information about their composers, descriptions of the composers' styles, who (in terms of their role and rank in society) sponsored music during the baroque and classical periods, and who sponsors music today. Students will compare the role that these classical composers played in their societies with the role occupied today's by rap, rock, and pop composers and performers. Students can find some of this information in the school or classroom library. The teacher will also encourage students to look for information on the Internet. Following are Web sites that contain excellent information (at the time of this writing):

- http://www.menc.org (the National Association for Music Education)
- http://www.essentialsofmusic.com/composer/composers.html (biographical information about composers)
- http://www.classical.net (composer biographies with links to other sites and lists of works)

Producing the Music Videos

After the class has listened to and discussed the work of at least eight composers, each team will choose its composer and the musical selection for its video and do the biographical research. At this point, the teacher will give teams time to brainstorm their lyrics, do a rough draft of the biographical booklet, and produce sample layouts for the advertising poster. The class also will need time to draw a timeline on a long strip of paper. Students will need to measure the strip's length and determine the number of years to be used in the timeline to calculate the scale (inches per year) of the timeline. Once they know the scale, students will use markers and a straight edge to draw the timeline. The scale for this timeline needs to be large enough to allow room to write in the composers' names. A portion of the finished timeline could look like the one shown in Figure 3.4.

The teacher will give teams time to review and approve the polished lyrics for their videos and to practice vocalizing these lyrics to the background music. The teacher can get tape or CD players from the music or media specialists in the school and will encourage teams to play their music very softly so that several teams can practice in a limited space. During this practice phase, teams also will plan their costumes and background decorations, or sets, for the final video production. Teams will edit and produce the presentation copy of the biographical booklet, and they will select a final poster layout and create the advertising poster.

The teacher and the student teams will probably need to schedule special times for actual production of the music videos. If students want to use the school auditorium, they will need to reserve a time when they can use that facility. The school's media specialist can help set up the videotaping equipment and show students how to use it. The teacher or the media specialist will want to be available to coach and help students during taping. The teacher will announce the date by which all videos must be ready for the final presentation and will help teams adjust the filming schedule so that all teams can meet the deadline.

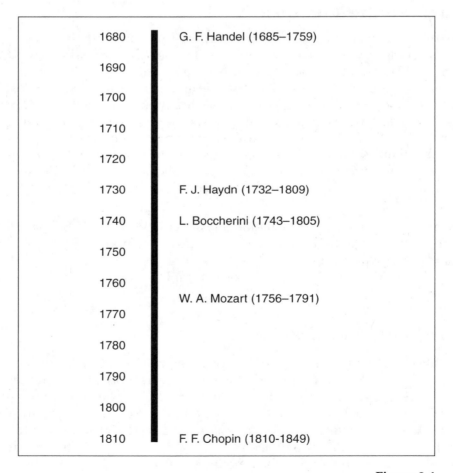

Figure 3.4

THE PRESENTATION

The teacher and students may decide that they want to invite parents, school administrators, or other teachers and students to attend the presentation performances of the music videos. They will design an invitation to announce the event (see Figure 3.5).

Members of the class will greet their guests, usher them to seats, and invite them to share in refreshments during the intermission. The teacher and students will discuss what happens at movie premieres and decide how they want to manage the formal presentation performance.

Before the premiere, each team will be scheduled for its order of appearance in the presentation. The class will prepare a program for the audience that includes, for each music video, the title of the video, the featured composer, the names of the team members, and the name of the featured musical selection. Ushers will give programs to audience members during seating.

As each team takes its turn, the Conductor will introduce the team members by name and role; announce the video's title, the composer's name, and the musical selection; and explain why the team chose that composer and music as its focus. The Correspondent/Poet and Dry Cell/Composer will summarize the biographical booklet, and the Conductor will present and describe the advertising poster. After this introduction, the team will show the music video and then answer audience members' questions about the video's content, the choice of lyrics, the composer, and what the students have learned about the connection between music and enhanced learning. The teacher, classmates, and other audience members will help each team celebrate success with applause and bravos.

You are invited

to attend a

PREMIER SCREENING

of music videos featuring

the lives of classical and

baroque composers.

Presented by the Sixth-Grade Students

Friday, April 20, 2007

12:30 p.m. to 3:30 p.m.

(with an intermission)

RSVP by April 16

Figure 3.5

THE REFLECTION

After the presentation performances, the posters, booklets, and videos will be on display in the classroom. The teacher will give each team several large sticky notes, and teams will perform a gallery walk, visiting each set of performance materials, writing a positive comment about the presentation on a sticky note, and placing the sticky note on the performance poster. At the conclusion of the gallery walk, teams will collect the sticky notes on their posters, read the comments, reflect on a series of questions (see "Team Reflection Questions" at the end of this chapter), and discuss their thoughts.

Students will have been keeping individual listening logs in which they record musical pieces they listen to and rate them according to their listening preferences. The teacher will instruct students to add information to this log for the rest of the school year. The teacher will be playing music as students learn new information and reflect on their learnings and will suggest that students listen to classical and baroque music outside of class. The teacher will ask students to include information about these musical experiences in their listening logs. (See "Listening Log" for a sample entry.) Teachers will tell their students that they will find and play classical or baroque selections in class that the students request.

In addition, each student will transfer what he or she has learned about rhythms in nonmusical settings by jotting down individual reflections twice each week for the month following the video presentation. (See "Rhythms in My Life Today" for a sample entry.) As students discover the rhythms that exist in everyday activities, they will become more aware of the effect of these rhythms on their emotions, and they will become better at choosing helpful background sounds as they study and learn.

Reflection

TEAM REFLECTION
Team Reflection Questions

What were we asked to do in this performance learning task?

What do we think we did well?

What do our classmates say we did well?

What would we improve next time?

Our top three learnings about our composer (or classical music in general) are

On a scale from 1 (low) to 5 (high), our enjoyment of classical music is a _____ because

Reflection

INDIVIDUAL REFLECTIONS
Listening Log

Composer	Music Selection	Personal Enjoyment
J. S. Bach	Bist Du Bei Mir	4
W. A. Mozart	"Jupiter" Symphony (molto allegro)	5
G. F. Handel	Water Music Overture	4
A. Vivaldi	The Four Seasons: Spring: Danza Pastorale	4

Rhythms in My Life Today

Rhythm (Source)	Pacing	Associated Feelings
uumph, uumph, uumph (tires on the road)	andante	hurry, scurry, tense
tick-tock/tick-tock/tick-tock (Mickey Mouse wall clock)	largo	restful, peaceful
alub, alub, alub, alub (heartbeat after gym class)	andante	run, play, happy, excited

4

Making
Sense of Stories

THE AUDIENCE

Grade Level

Enhancing student literacy, the ability of students to read for deep understanding and insight, write and speak clearly, and listen attentively, is a goal of all educators, kindergarten through high school and beyond. Because this activity asks students to write questions that target higher-order critical and creative thinking skills, it is appropriate for students in Grades 5 through high school and beyond. Teachers of younger students can modify the task by requiring fewer questions that target these higher levels of thinking.

Diverse Learners

Careful assigning of students to cooperative learning teams can result in maximum learning for all. See the Preface for suggestions about team roles and responsibilities. For this performance learning activity, the Correspondent will collect and organize questions written by individual team members, the Conductor will edit the questions and speak for the team during construction of the whole-class people search, and the Dry Cell will check teammates for information and understandings learned by reading the story. All team members will write questions to contribute to the final people search. By carefully matching each student to a role, the teacher will encourage feelings of relaxed alertness that lead to deeper learning (Caine et al., 2005).

Before teachers introduce this activity to students, they will look over the task development chart and the performance rubric to decide which tasks are appropriate

for their grade level or for individual students. Using the rubric will allow the teacher and each student to differentiate the curriculum by tailoring the activity to the child's level of readiness (Tomlinson, 1999). Teachers will also need to adapt the activity for the developmental level of their students.

THE PERFORMANCE

Reading comprehension is a function of the attentiveness of the reader. If readers' eyes and minds are focused on the story in front of them, they will probably be able to discuss its characters, setting, and plot. A reader whose attention is engaged will be able to infer the story's theme and the social principles or beliefs associated with the characters' actions. The intent reader may want to predict the unwritten sequel to the story and support those predictions with evidence from the text. As focused readers work through a story, they often make connections with other stories, comparing and contrasting the literary pieces. Robert Sylwester (2006a) says that emotion and attention are the brain's cognitive activation systems. Csikszentmihalyi (2002) states that students want to learn when they are intrinsically motivated, and this condition exists when they find a task enjoyable. To secure the attention of student readers and to enhance intrinsic motivation, the teacher will give them a task that empowers them by asking them to identify key information from a story and to analyze clues to determine its theme and underlying principles.

As they do this performance learning task, students will read a story and write a people search to use as a postreading review tool. A people search is an interactive classroom strategy that gets students moving around the room, forming temporary partnerships, and exchanging information about a focus topic. To promote higher-order thinking, the teacher will give students a copy of the Three-Story Intellect diagram (Figure 4.3) and tell them to use second- and third-story verbs to write two-thirds of their questions. Students also need to be able to write complete answers for all of the questions they ask.

By using this assignment structure, the teacher creates the expectation that students will understand the story. As students ask and answer first-story questions, they demonstrate their knowledge of the story's facts. Students demonstrate their abilities to infer theme, values, beliefs, and future actions as they write and answer second- and third-story questions. The higher-level questions also could involve comparing this story with others students have read or with their experiences from everyday life.

The people search writing assignment will focus the students' attention on the reading task and help them improve their reading comprehension. Because this is an active reading task in which students are creating their own questions about the story, students who are engaged in the task may find themselves in a state of flow (Csikszentmihalyi, 1990). This performance learning task incorporates many of the elements Csikszentmihalyi says define this highly involved, positive state. Students who are doing the task will have a clear goal, which is to write and answer the people search questions. Because students are familiar with the kinds of questions the teacher typically asks about a story, they will find the challenge of the activity closely aligns with their skills. Students will begin this task with the goal of writing the people search, so they will receive continuous feedback as the task progresses because they can see the questions and answers they are compiling.

Students will be unconcerned about threat or danger as they do the task because they are creating the reading comprehension assessment tool. Students often feel intimidated as they read because of the judgmental evaluation they know will come at the end of the task. They focus on guessing what the teacher wants them to know, so they concentrate on the details of the story and spend little time analyzing the central theme. When students write the questions, they focus on the activity of question writing and answering, and if the teacher has specified the use of second- and third-story verbs in their questions, the students will look for patterns, core issues and themes, and connections to other stories or everyday life.

To provide an audience for this task, students will ask members of another class to read their target story, do the people search as their review activity, and provide feedback about the effectiveness of the people search in reinforcing learning. Just as the people search helps students review the facts and concepts from the story they read, comments from members of another class will facilitate a review of the writing process and the use of this review tool. Jensen (1995) notes that frequent feedback is a vital key to boosting learning and intelligence. By reviewing the story and the process, students will acquire more complete knowledge and understanding of the content they learned and the skills by which they learned it.

The Prompt

After the students have read a story, the teacher will tell them that they will use an interactive strategy called a people search to review what they have read. Each student will receive a copy of the people search questions (see Figure 4.1), and the teacher will explain the procedure.

Students will learn that as they do a people search, they will be collecting information and insights from their classmates. The teacher and students will examine guidelines for doing the people search (see Figure 4.2), and the guidelines will be posted in the room for future reference.

The teacher will stress that a classmate may give and explain only one answer to a person, so the students will need to contact as many classmates as there are people search items. After checking to be sure that students understand the procedure, the teacher will ask students to do the people search.

At the end of the allotted time, the teacher will ask all students to regroup and will facilitate a discussion of the answers to the questions. Students will analyze the structure of the people search by answering questions such as, "Did you take more time to answer some questions than others? Which questions required longer answers? Why do you think you wanted more time to answer those questions?" The teacher and class will take some time to identify the questions that students spent more time answering.

Next, the teacher will give each student a copy of the Three-Story Intellect diagram (see Figure 4.3) and explain the concept of one-story, two-story, and three-story verbs. The teacher will tell the students that questions using first-story verbs are fact- and information-collecting questions that test recall of details from the reading.

A Playful People Search: *Jumanji*

Find someone who can respond to each of the following questions or instructions. Ask that person to tell you the response and to sign this sheet next to the appropriate question or statement. A person can sign only one time.

1. The title is the name of two things in the book. What are they? _____	2. Get two different people to sign this one. Who likes to eat pumpkin pie? What actress had Munchkin friends? _____ _____
3. Sketch two clock faces. Set the hands on the first clock face for the time at the beginning of the story. Set the hands on the second clock face for the time at the end of the story. _____	4. Do a sequence cartoon that pictures the action in the story using the house's floor plan as a map. _____
	5. Rank the adventures in the story from least scary to most scary. _____
6. "We interrupt this story to . . ." What happens when the parents come home before the children finish the game? _____	7. The Jumanji game is like [a kind of food] because both [have these three things in common]. _____
8. What quote from another story best sums up the theme in this story? Explain your choice. _____	9. Write the ending for Jumanji 2. Tell why you chose this ending. _____

Figure 4.1

Doing a People Search

1. Get out of your chair. Move around the room.

2. Make eye contact with a classmate. Smile and address the person by his or her first name.

3. Say, "Do you need someone to answer number [one or two . . . pick a number]? I can do that!"

4. Give and explain the answer. Ask the person to paraphrase what you said to check for understanding. Sign the person's people search sheet.

5. Ask the person to answer and explain a question for which you need a signature. Paraphrase and get the signature you need.

6. Say, "Thank you," and move on.

7. Be ready to contribute to a class discussion of the answers to the questions when the people search time has expired.

Figure 4.2

Questions using second-story verbs are information-processing questions that encourage analysis of the reading. Third-story questions stimulate evaluation of the reading and encourage comparison with other selections, creation of new endings, and/or prediction of sequels.

Then the teacher will ask students to identify the levels of the people search questions. Students can do this by focusing on the verbs in the questions. The teacher will ask, "How does the question level relate to the length of time involved in answering a question? Do you see any patterns? What relationship do you see?" Students will say that the questions on which they spent more time were second- and third-story questions. Finally, the teacher will ask, "Why are some first-story questions good to have on a people search?" This will help students understand that inference, analysis, and prediction must be rooted in the solid, factual base provided by questions that use the first-story verbs.

The teacher will ask students to reflect on the people search review strategy using de Bono's (1976) PMI, as shown in Figure 4.4: "To review our learnings from story reading, how is using a people search helpful (plus), not helpful (minus), or interesting?"

After the students and teacher have finished the debriefing, the teacher will tell the students that they will begin this task by reading a new story and writing the people search review as they read. In small teams, students will use their individually written people searches to create a team composite. The whole class will use these team people searches to create a consensus version. Students will use the people search to review the story. They will evaluate and revise the people search, and then they will ask members of another class to read the story, use the consensus people search as a review activity, and give feedback about the quality of the people search and the effectiveness of this strategy to review learnings from a reading selection. A people search form is in the reproducibles section at the end of this book.

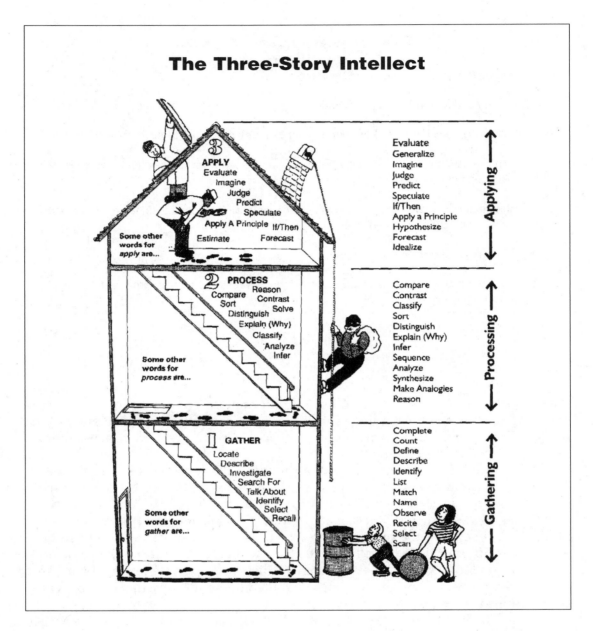

Figure 4.3

SOURCE: *From Start Them Thinking: A Handbook of Classroom Strategies for Early Years,* by Robin Fogarty and Kay Opeka, copyright 1998 by IRI/Skylight Publishing, Inc., p. xvi.

The Vision

Before students do their active reading task, the teacher will show examples of people searches and ask them, "Which of these people searches would you rather do? Which might be the most fun? What are your reasons for your answers?"

Fogarty (1997) suggests that effective people search items "spirit" key issues through the back door. She says that students will be more engaged in people searches that are focused and fun. The teacher can demonstrate this by giving students examples of both serious (see Figure 4.5) and playful (see Figure 4.1) people searches.

Plus	Minus	Interesting

Figure 4.4

A Serious People Search: *Jumanji*

1. What does the title of the book refer to?

2. State the names of the main characters.

3. Identify the time of day when the story takes place.

4. Outline the events in the story.

5. Describe the event in the story that scared you the most.

6. Explain why Mother and Father didn't believe the children's story about what happened while they were gone.

7. Forecast what Mother and Father would have found when they returned if the children had not finished the game.

8. What is the theme of this story?

9. Predict what will happen in the sequel to this story.

Figure 4.5

The teacher could ask students, "If emotion drives attention, which of these people searches would you find more emotionally engaging? For what reasons? How would doing this people search help you understand the story better and remember it longer? What does this tell you about writing a people search of your own?" The teacher and students will discuss the answers to these questions before the students do the performance learning task.

The Standards

The teacher will give each student a copy of the task development chart for this performance learning task (see Figure 4.6) after students have completed the initial people search. Because students may become so engrossed with writing the people search for the new story that they lose sight of the big picture, the teacher will use the task development chart to remind students that their primary goal is enhanced reading comprehension. Writing the people search is one way to facilitate higher-order analysis of reading selections because students must look for central patterns and themes in order to ask second- and third-story questions.

Each student will need a copy of the rubric for this performance learning task (see Figure 4.7) to monitor personal reading comprehension and to continuously evaluate and improve his or her people search. The teacher will work with students to help them become more skilled in asking second- and third-story questions and to ensure that they have a firm first-story base of facts upon which to build inferences and predictions.

THE COACHING CONTEXT

Preview

The first people search review that students use will be created by the teacher. Before students read a story, the teacher will suggest they look for a theme and will give some examples: practice what you preach; finish what you start; explore new horizons; help friends in need. The teacher also may ask students to tie the theme or characters' actions to social values or beliefs—for example, integrity, loyalty, compassion, or equal justice. To ease assessment anxiety, the teacher will tell students that they will be doing an interactive, whole-class review of the story and will briefly describe the process: "I'll give you some questions about the story. You'll talk with classmates about the answers. Then we'll all discuss the answers. Finally, I'll ask each of you to individually reflect on what you read. I think you'll like this. I hope you'll have fun!"

Students will read the story individually. Then the teacher will give each student a copy of the people search review for the story and explain the people search procedure. After students do the people search and the class discusses the answers, each student will do an individual written review and reflection about the story (see Figure 4.8).

(Text continued on page 48)

Jumanji **Review and Reflections**

Here's a quick summary of the story:

I think the theme is _____ because _____

What I liked best about the story is _____ because _____

What I'd like to see changed is _____ because _____

The people search review helped me by _____

Figure 4.8

Task Development Chart: Making Sense of Stories

Performance Tasks	Developmental Levels	Curriculum Standards
Read a story and do a teacher-written people search review. Practice the rules for doing a people search. Inspect the people search structure for first-, second-, and third-story intellect questions.	**Novice** Identifies characters and some actions in a story. Sequences actions and summarizes plot with difficulty. Cannot identify central theme, concepts, principles, or patterns or connect with other reading. Uses mostly first-story questions.	**Language Arts: Reading** Check and clarify for understanding by rereading and retelling. Use story information to ask and answer questions and make predictions. Analyze text for point of view, theme, and important principles.
Read a new story. Write a people search while doing the reading. Include first-story fact finding; second-story analyzing, explaining, comparing, and inferring; and third-story predicting and evaluating.	**Advanced Beginner** Identifies main characters and their actions. Sequences actions with 75 percent accuracy. Forgets some of the key events in the plot. Cannot identify central theme, concepts, or patterns or connect with other reading. Uses second- and third-story questions 25 percent of time.	Compare and contrast with other stories. Summarize information from a story using a variety of graphic organizers (e.g., five fingers for who, what, when, where, why; Venn diagrams to compare and contrast; sequence charts or chain links to summarize plot; right angle for fact and feeling or action and feeling, etc.).
Teams: Use individual people searches to write composites. Class: Do gallery walk to produce consensus people search. Use people search to review the story.	**Competent User** Identifies main characters. Remembers and sequences at least 75 percent of the key action in story. Cannot verbalize theme. Compares with at least one other story and gives reasons. Uses second- and third-story questions 50 percent of time.	**Language Arts: Writing** Write questions using complete sentence structures and clear syntax. Use precise, descriptive vocabulary in questions and answers. Edit and revise questions for word choice, spelling, punctuation, and syntax.
Individuals: Write story test, including summary of plot and characters, discussion of theme and values, and analysis of question writing for comprehension strategy.	**Proficient Performer** Identifies and describes most characters and summarizes plot accurately. Identifies the theme and at least one other story with the same theme. Identifies at least one contrasting story. Uses second- and third-story questions 50 percent of time.	**Thinking Skills** Ask questions at a variety of cognitive levels. Demonstrate critical thinking skills of analyzing, sequencing, and summarizing. Demonstrate creative thinking skills of brainstorming, inferring, and predicting.
Audience Class: Read the story, do the people search review, and give feedback. Performance Class: Review and analyze feedback to sharpen questioning skills. Individuals: Use question-asking strategies while reading.	**Expert** Describes characters vividly and sketches plot. Supports theme with underlying principles or beliefs. Compares and contrasts with several other stories using plot, theme, and characters. Uses second- and third-story questions at least 60 percent of time.	**Social Studies** Connect the theme of the story to the values and beliefs of the culture that produced the story.

Figure 4.6

45

Performance Rubric: Making Sense of Stories

Developmental Level / Performance	Novice	Advanced Beginner	Competent User	Proficient Performer	Expert
Identify Characters and Plot	Names main characters. Forgets other characters. Can't link characters to action or sequence of story events.	Knows main characters and at least one other. Forgets relationships among characters. Links characters to action with 50 percent accuracy.	Knows most of the characters. Correctly identifies 50 percent of the relationships among characters. Links characters to action with 75 percent accuracy.	Knows most of the characters and their relationships. Links characters to action with 75 percent accuracy. Gives complete plot summary.	Knows most of the characters and their relationships. Links characters to action with 90 percent accuracy. Gives complete plot summary.
Infer Theme, Principles, and Sequel	Sees no underlying beliefs or principles behind actions or events. "When the story is over, it's over! What do you mean, what's next?"	Vaguely perceives beliefs behind actions. Sees no principles illustrated by the story. Creates a new story for which there is no evidence in the original.	Ties characters' actions to core beliefs or values. Vaguely senses universal principle illustrated by story. Writes a sequel faithful to the characters' beliefs.	Illustrates accurate analysis of core beliefs of characters and principles as evidenced in the unfolding story. Writes a sequel faithful to the characters' personalities; not so strong on events.	Analyzes beliefs and principles accurately; provides evidence to support analysis. Writes a sequel that could have been written by the original author!
Recognize Patterns; Connect to Other Stories	Makes no connections; forms no patterns. "A story is a story!" Does not compare to other stories.	"*Winnie the Pooh* is like *Three Little Pigs* because they both have pigs!" Provides superficial connections. Compares only; does not contrast.	Sees some story patterns: family relationships, actions such as caring for pets, events such as being frightened or happy. Names a few stories with similar patterns.	Sees some story patterns: families, actions, and events. Names a few other stories with similar or contrasting patterns.	Sees some story patterns: families, actions, events, beliefs, or principles such as compassion, respect for others, equal rights. Names several stories with similar or contrasting patterns.

Figure 4.7

Use Writing Skills	Uses few complete sentences. Uses subject/verb disagreements more than 50 percent of time. Leaves six or more misspellings. Uses vague, imprecise vocabulary: "The ending stinks," not "I didn't like the ending because ..."	Uses a few complete sentences. Uses subject/verb disagreements 30 percent to 40 percent of time. Leaves four or five misspellings. Uses vague, imprecise vocabulary: "The ending rules," not "I liked the ending because ..."	Uses complete sentences 50 percent to 60 percent of time. Uses subject/verb disagreements 15 percent to 30 percent of time. Leaves two or three misspellings. Uses more precise vocabulary: "The character was persistent," not "The character was way cool."	Uses complete sentences 70 percent to 90 percent of time. Uses subject/verb disagreements 5 percent to 10 percent of time. Leaves one misspelling or none. Chooses precise words consistently; describes events colorfully.	Uses complete sentences 90 percent of time. Uses correct subject/verb agreements almost always. Leaves no misspellings. Chooses precise words consistently. Describes events and characters colorfully and vividly.
Sense and Ask Questions	Needs prompting to write any questions. Does not remember who, what, when, where, or why.	Remembers who, what, when, where, and why. Asks second- and third-story questions only with prompting: "Is it better?" but not "How is it better?"	Uses five fingers to cue who, what, when, where, and why. Asks some second-story questions: Compare this with ..., "Why do you think the character needed to ...?"	Uses first-story answers to cue higher-level questions. Asks for analogy building. Asks for use of graphic organizers in answers.	Uses first-story answers to cue higher-level questions. Asks for analogy building and use of graphic organizers in answers. Digs out patterns, themes, attitudes, and values.

Figure 4.7

(Text continued from page 44)

The Set-Up

After students do the teacher-written people search review, the teacher will distribute copies of the Three-Story Intellect diagram, and the teacher and the students will analyze the level of each question. First, the teacher will explain the active reading assignment. Students will read a new story, and each student will write a people search review as he or she reads the story. Second, students will meet in small teams and write a team composite people search review. Third, the whole class will view and discuss the team versions and reach consensus on a people search review of the story. The teacher will assemble the questions and make copies of the people search, and the students will do the people search review of the story. Fourth, the students will ask another class to read the story, review it using their people search, and give them feedback about the effectiveness of the review and the quality of the questions. Finally, students will reflect on the experience and its impact on their reading comprehension.

Other Sources of Help

Some students may want to know more about reading for comprehension or other active reading strategies. The teacher can help students find Web sites that contain information and links to other sources of ideas. A search engine will give many possible Web sites for the search terms "reading comprehension," "reading strategies," "improving reading skills," or other key phrases.

Doing the Task

The teacher will suggest that students begin the writing before they begin the reading by creating some first-story information-gathering questions. When they read any story, students will want to pay attention to characters and setting, including geographical details and time period. To summarize a story, students will want to remember key events and the order in which they occurred in the story. If students have a rough draft of their "who, what, when, where, and why" questions written before they begin reading the story, they can collect their answers as they read. The teacher will assign the story, and students will write their people searches as they read.

After students have written their individual people searches for the new story, small teams of students will use the individual versions to prepare composite people searches. Each team will write its people search on chart paper and post the people search in a designated classroom location. Teams will do a gallery walk to read and discuss these people searches and compile suggestions for a whole-class people search. The teacher will facilitate a discussion during which students will reach consensus on this final version of the people search. The teacher will make a copy-ready master, photocopy it, give each student a copy, and direct the class review of the story.

Improving the Product

After the class has used the people search to review the story, small teams will reflect on the product and how they believe it could be improved. They may use Mrs. Potter's questions (Fogarty, 2001) to guide the reflection:

- What were we asked to do?

- What did we do well?
- What would we do differently next time?
- What help do we need in improving this product?

The class will meet to discuss and approve revisions to the people search, and the teacher will produce a copy-ready master. The students will ask members of another class to read the story, use the people search to review the story, and give feedback about the effectiveness of the review process and the quality of the people search itself.

THE PRESENTATION

The students will invite students in another class to be the presentation audience. The students in the presentation class will outline the process of writing a people search and explain how becoming question askers helped them focus on the central issues and theme of the story. They also will describe how this process helped them feel more confident and less threatened by the evaluation process. They may want to explain how these positive emotions and feelings of safety enhanced their content learning.

The students in the audience class will read the story, and the presentation class members will direct the use of the people search as a review tool. Following the review, each student in the audience class will provide feedback by answering a set of questions (see Figure 4.9).

People Search Feedback

Here's a short summary of the story and its theme:

Here's what I learned about the reading and questioning process:

A question that I still have about the process is:

I'd give the questions on this people search a [check one]

_____ thumbs up   _____ thumbs sideways   _____ thumbs down

because _____

Figure 4.9

THE REFLECTION

The presentation class students will review the feedback provided by students in the audience class. The teacher and students will discuss answers to the questions the audience class members had about the reading and the questioning process to clarify their own thinking about these ideas. They will examine the ratings of the people search questions and record this information on a large sheet of chart paper as a whole-class reflection. Students may refer to this whole-class reflection as they engage in question-asking assignments in the future. Each individual also will do a personal reflection using questions and sentence starters as a guide.

Recent research shows that reading for pleasure is an infrequent activity for most children and adults. One reason for this may be the stress that some students feel as they read without direction and with no definite idea of what they are expected to learn. By using a safe, low-risk question-asking strategy to focus reading, teachers may help their students have more fun reading and may encourage reading for pleasure as a lifelong activity.

Reflection

WHOLE-CLASS REFLECTION
The Quality of Our Question Writing

What we're doing well is

What we want to improve is

Things we can do to improve are

Here are some sources of help:

INDIVIDUAL REFLECTION
My Understanding and Enjoyment of Reading

By asking questions about the story as I read it, I understood this story

☐ Worse than usual   ☐ Same as usual   ☐ Better than usual

By writing the test as I read the story, I felt

☐ Stressed   ☐ OK   ☐ Relaxed

I enjoyed this reading assignment

☐ Less than usual   ☐ Same as usual   ☐ More than usual

because

I hope we get to write the test when we read other stories because

PART II

Intermediate Performances

5

"... To Form a More Perfect Classroom"

THE AUDIENCE

Grade Level

Federal law passed in 2004 requires all schools that receive federal funding to teach a short course on the Constitution to all students on Constitution Day, September 17. Many states require students to demonstrate knowledge about local, state, and federal governments before graduating from middle school or high school. Students typically take in these courses in Grades 7–12. As students study political systems, they can develop a deeper understanding of how governments are structured by writing a classroom constitution. Teacher and students can find a wealth of information about writing and implementing constitutions by using an Internet search engine such as Google or Dogpile to search for "writing a constitution," "classroom constitutions," and similar phrases.

Diverse Learners

Careful assigning of students to cooperative learning teams can result in maximum learning for all. See the Preface for suggestions about team roles and responsibilities. For this performance learning activity, the Correspondent will record the final version of the team's section of the constitution, the Conductor will present the constitution section to the rest of the class, and the Dry Cell will manage and defuse conflicts that arise as teammates discuss their ideas. All team members will take turns answering questions about the constitution section following presentation to the class. By carefully matching each student to a role, the teacher encourages feelings of relaxed alertness that lead to deeper learning (Caine et al., 2005).

Before introducing this activity to students, teachers will look over the task development chart and the performance rubric to decide which tasks are appropriate for their grade level or for individual students. Each student will, for example, keep a constitutional journal, and the performance level targets and ways of recording information for individual students will be different. Using the rubric will allow the teacher and each student to differentiate the curriculum by tailoring the activity to the child's level of readiness (Tomlinson, 1999). Teachers will also need to tailor the activity to fit the developmental level of their students.

THE PERFORMANCE

Every social organization, whether it is a clan, state, government, society, or extended family, has a system of fundamental beliefs and rules under which it functions. This system of rules and principles, written or unwritten, is the constitution of the organization. Before students study the constitutions of the United States and their home state, they can experience the process of developing and writing a constitution. They will begin by identifying and formally stating the fundamental beliefs under which they want their classroom to function. Students then will write a classroom constitution that embodies and formalizes these ideals and principles. They will use this constitution to act as or elect a legislative body that will write the laws under which the classroom will operate. Finally, students will improve their constitution by adding amendments that safeguard the rights of individuals or groups. As students study the writing of the constitution of the United States, they will learn that their classroom constitution-writing process parallels the steps used by the authors of the federal constitution.

Students will experience this task as an ongoing, evolutionary process. Each student will keep a journal in which he or she records personal insights about the steps involved in the creation of a written constitution, discussions or disagreements with other students, methods the class used to manage conflict and resolve disagreements, and reflections on how the constitution-writing process has helped the student clarify his or her beliefs about individual rights and responsibilities, social principles and ideals, and government functions. The teacher will encourage each student to keep a journal using a format that is meaningful and comfortable for that individual.

For their final exhibition of learning, small teams of students will present what they have learned about writing a constitution to other classes in the school. They will explain the process by which they developed their final product and describe their understanding of what a constitution is and what it does. To connect this performance to the world beyond the school, teams will show how their process parallels the writing and evolution of the U.S. Constitution. Students can obtain insight into presenting a constitution to an audience by examining the book *Constitution Translated for Kids* (Travis, 2006). Because the book targets a young audience, its clear explanation of difficult material is a useful guide for student constitution writers as they plan their final presentations. Audience members will give feedback by saying what they learned from the presentation and how this learning helped them understand the function and importance of a constitution with regard to the efficient functioning of a society.

The Prompt

Students who do this performance learning task may have heard the term *constitution*, but they may not have a very clear understanding of what the word means. The teacher will give the class a definition, assign students to teams of three, and ask each team to brainstorm examples of written or unwritten constitutions and the groups they serve. Students may suggest that towns, states, and nations all have constitutions. They may not understand that clans, tribes, and families often operate under commonly accepted, unwritten systems of beliefs and rules that can be considered constitutions.

The teacher will suggest that a constitution helps a social group function more efficiently because the constitution establishes procedures and rules for frequently encountered situations. The teacher will say that it is important for students to understand the process of developing this kind of document because they all live in a state and a country that have formal, written constitutions. The teacher also will tell students that to become informed citizens, they will learn about the state and federal constitutions and the writing of the U.S. Constitution as they work toward a classroom constitution.

In introducing the task, the teacher will describe the personal journal each student will keep, the steps in the constitution-development process, and the final presentation to another class in the school. The teacher will make arrangements for doing this presentation before students begin the task. Teacher and students will brainstorm the elements that are part of making a quality presentation, and the teacher will incorporate the results of the brainstorm into the rubric for the performance task (see Figure 5.2).

The teacher will give the students a list of the ideas they will discuss in the presentation:

- Steps in the constitution-development process
- Clarification of principles and beliefs underlying the constitution
- Function and role of the constitution in helping a social group function more efficiently
- Constitutional evolution and improvement over time

The Vision

Students will want to know how the leaders of a society agree on ideas and write a constitution. Several good books appropriate for different reading levels tell this story, and the teacher may want to have students read and discuss these books before they begin the performance task. Students can view the movie *1776* (Warner Brothers, 1972), which features the problems and disagreements encountered by the founding fathers during the writing of the Declaration of Independence. This film classic gives a musical look at the ways in which the writers of the Declaration of Independence overcame personal differences to establish a common vision of a nation. The teacher also will share with students excerpts from the diaries of the writers of the U.S. Constitution and ask students to comment on what they learn from these passages. Students may be surprised to learn that the country's founding fathers did not always agree with each other and that they often did not particularly like each other, and yet they still found ways to agree on the best course for the country.

The teacher also will tell students that the writers of the U.S. Constitution knew they had created an imperfect document and that, before the original Constitution was ratified, the first 10 amendments were envisioned. They can give students a list of the amendments, the dates of their ratification, and their purposes to show that, at its best, a constitution is an evolving, changing document that reflects the ideals and attitudes of the society that produces it.

The Standards

As students do this task, they will be learning about the historical development of the U.S. Constitution and their state's constitution and writing a constitution for use in their own classroom. They will want to take some care in weaving together the threads of their learning to form some key concepts: what a constitution is, what it does, and how the beliefs of a society determine the contents of its constitution and its form of government.

Early in the performance learning task, the teacher will give each student a copy of the task development chart (see Figure 5.1). Using the task development chart will help students appreciate what they have learned and what they can do well, and it will assist them as they look for ways to improve their performance and become more adept constitutional scholars.

The performance rubric (see Figure 5.2) for this task indicates its separate threads. Students will demonstrate their understanding of constitutional concepts they have learned through participating in the process of identifying their core beliefs and deciding what form of government and what laws are appropriate for their classroom society. Their journals will be key tools in processing their knowledge, and their preparation for the final presentation will help them review what they have learned and clarify the concepts in their own minds. Students can self-evaluate the quality of their learning and preparation for the final performance using the task rubric, and this self-evaluation can lead to higher-quality presentations and the formation of deeper understandings and more complex concepts.

THE COACHING CONTEXT

Gathering Start-Up Information

The teacher and students will use several information-gathering strategies simultaneously during the early phase of this activity. After assigning students to small teams, the teacher will use a combination of print, video, and online resources to help students acquire valuable background for the task. The teacher may choose to have the entire class read the same book or have different teams read different works and summarize them for the class. Young readers will find a variety of books on this topic such as *Constitution Translated for Kids* (Travis, 2006) and *Shhh! We're Writing the Constitution* (Fritz, 1997). After watching sections of *1776*, the teacher and students can list techniques for defusing conflicts and reaching consensus and post them on a chart in the room (see Figure 5.3). The Dry Cells in all teams will need a copy of these conflict and consensus managing techniques to refer to as they perform their roles.

A number of Internet Web sites contain valuable pointers about the process of writing a constitution. Students and the teacher can find information by searching for "writing a constitution," "classroom constitutions," or similar phrases.

(Text continued on page 62)

Task Development Chart: ". . . To Form a More Perfect Classroom"

Performance Tasks	Developmental Levels	Curriculum Standards
Brainstorm: What are our core beliefs and principles? What are the rights and responsibilities of individuals? What is the "rule of law"? What is a constitution? Form this concept. Must it be a written document?	**Novice** Unaware of personal beliefs or system of principles. Vaguely aware of government as "them." Cannot define "constitution." Gives no examples of written or unwritten constitutions. Displays no conflict management or consensus skills: "My way or the highway!"	**Social Studies** Identify fundamental beliefs for social organizations: respect for others, individual rights and responsibilities, fairness, equity, justice. Recognize role of laws in effective functioning of society: to promote common good and maintain order and security. Explain key ideals of representative democracy: individual dignity, liberty, justice, rule of law. Trace historic origins of social principles and ideals. Show how constitutions change over time with interpretation and amendment.
Decide on format for the constitution. (Use Internet resources.) Small Teams: Draft assigned sections. Whole Class: Discuss, debate, reach consensus. Assemble and adopt the constitution. Elect team representatives to house of representatives.	**Advanced Beginner** Quotes "golden rule" or other memorized statement of beliefs or principles. Names some local elected officials. Knows a constitution has something to do with laws. Knows about written constitutions. Listens to differing points of view without agreeing.	**Language Arts** Read about writing a constitution and summarize reading selections. Write constitution and amendments demonstrating precise use of vocabulary and writing conventions. Speak persuasively. Listen with focus: summarize, paraphrase, ask speaker for clarification.
Whole Class: Operate under rules of constitution. Identify unclear areas. Test amendment procedures: representatives draft an amendment, take back to teams, teams vote to adopt or kill amendment.	**Competent User** States core beliefs in own language. Names local officials, governor, and U.S. president. Knows separation of powers and U.S. Bill of Rights. Gives examples of unwritten constitutions. Listens to and may agree with different viewpoints.	**Mathematics** Solve ratio and proportion calculations to determine number of representatives each team can send to the legislative house. Calculate this for legislative houses of varying sizes to determine ideal size to use for the class.
Record insights about the process and key interactions with classmates, differences and disagreements, means of reaching consensus, beliefs about role of government and rights of individuals.	**Proficient Performer** Discusses core beliefs and principles. Knows names of many local, state, and national elected officials. Explains powers of executive, judicial, and legislative branches and applies to clans, tribes, and families. Demonstrates consensus-reaching skills.	**Library Media and Technology** Find print materials that are good sources of information. Locate Web sites that provide helpful information. Evaluate information sources for accuracy and helpfulness. Communicate with national senators, congressional representative, and other elected officials at http://www.congress.org/main.html.
Research writing of state and federal constitutions and their key points. Communicate results of constitution-writing experience and study of historical events to another class.	**Expert** Discusses core beliefs and principles and need for laws. Communicates with elected officials to make views known. Gives examples of executive, judicial, and legislative actions. Gives detailed explanations of unwritten constitutions. Helps others learn consensus-reaching skills.	

Figure 5.1

Performance Rubric: ". . . To Form a More Perfect Classroom"

Developmental Level / Performance	Novice	Advanced Beginner	Competent User	Proficient Performer	Expert
Develop a Model of Democracy	Survival of the strongest. No laws or rules. "Every man for himself." Little trust or respect.	Rule by the strongest. Rules serve the strongest. One king and many peasants; little trust or respect between ruler and ruled.	Cooperation among members of society. Unwritten rules protect everyone. Group compliance overseen with rules.	Elected leaders. Written rules based on common beliefs. Much duplication of functions of society.	Elected leaders have special roles or functions. Written rules based on common beliefs. System constantly evolves.
Participate in the Process	Monopolizes discussion time. Does not attempt to see others' points of view; argues, becomes angry. Does only what he or she wants; displays no teamwork skills.	Bosses others in the team. Meets disagreement with sarcasm and criticism. Assigns all of the work to others.	Takes turns during discussions. Listens when others disagree; seldom accepts others' point of view. Does his or her share of the work.	Rotates leadership with teammates. Listens, paraphrases, asks for clarification; will change mind. Knows team sinks or swims together.	Nominates others for leadership. Enjoys seeing different points of view. Accepts ideas of others. Displays skill at team give-and-take.
Write a Constitutional Journal	Writes few entries; most days missing. Focuses on gossip and personality conflicts. Does not reflect on beliefs, process, concepts.	Writes entries for at least 50 percent of days. Focuses on "what I did": lists activities and actions. Does not reflect on beliefs, process, concepts.	Writes entries for at least 80 percent of days. Gives some insights into the process; describes concepts. Notes interactions, conflicts, discussions with humor.	Writes entries for most days. Shows insight into concepts and classmates. Reflects on beliefs, rights, government roles. Notes interactions with insight and humor.	Writes entries for most days. Shows deep understanding of classmates and concepts. Reflects deeply on beliefs, rights, and government role. Provides good commentary on conflict management and reaching consensus.

Figure 5.2

Understand the Process	Displays no insight. Thinks a constitution just happens. Cannot explain or repeat steps independently.	Sees a little of it. Knows that ideals and laws are connected somehow. Doesn't bridge to the written document.	Sees how ideals and principles bridge to laws. Doesn't see evolution of society as laws are tested. Remembers to start with ideals and then write.	Understands that laws are rooted in ideals. Knows laws can change over time. Does not see the ongoing cycle.	Shows clear vision of ongoing cycle: principles to drafting to testing to amending to aligning with principles and so on. Understands that strong governments constantly evolve.
Participate in Presentation	Hangs head. Mumbles. Does not invite audience participation. Uses no visuals.	Uses adequate volume. Reads from a script. Doesn't look up. Does not interact with audience. "Talking head."	Uses adequate volume, some inflection. Presents script as if memorized. Waits for audience to laugh at jokes. Acts rehearsed.	Uses good volume and inflection. Consults notes occasionally. Invites questions from audience; answers clearly. Acts as a teacher.	Uses good volume, tone, and inflection. Uses brief notes to keep on track. Does think-pair-share, etc. Honors ideas of audience. Acts as a facilitator.

Figure 5.2

Conflict-Defusing and Consensus-Reaching Techniques

We can manage conflict and reach consensus by

- Letting the speaker finish.
- Paraphrasing what the speaker has said (instead of contradicting).
- Finding ways to say "and" instead of "or" or "but."
- Saying, "Tell me what you know that I don't."
- Using "I" statements (e.g., I perceive, I think, I could, I want).
- Avoiding "you" statements (e.g., you think, you could, you know).
- Letting everyone who wants a say have one.
- Speaking pleasantly and politely.
- Taking time to reflect before voting.
- Agreeing to abide by the majority vote.

Figure 5.3

(Text continued from page 58)

Students will need to develop a format that will fit their needs. A format for a good constitution for a government unit often includes these items and sections:

- The name of the organization
- Membership requirements
- Election of officers
- Powers, duties, and qualifications of officers
- Composition of a rule-making body
- Election of members of this body
- Composition and selection of a rules-interpretation committee

Students will decide if they want to write separate articles dividing powers among branches of government and detailing ratification and amendment procedures. They may decide they want their constitution to include a preamble. The teacher can supplement any format that students design or find on the Internet with suggestions and examples of the formats of the federal and state constitutions. The U.S. Constitution and Bill of Rights, accompanied by explanations of these documents and teaching suggestions, are available online at http://www.usconstitution.net.

Before the class begins writing a constitution, one important decision it needs to make is whether the whole class will serve as the legislature or whether students will use proportional representation to elect members to a house of representatives. The teacher can use this discussion to introduce the idea that, in a system of proportional representation, the number of representatives to which a state is entitled depends on its population, and this is why having accurate procedures for taking a population count (census) is so important. For a single classroom, students and teacher may decide that the whole class will serve as the legislature.

To give students some insight into the usefulness of proportional representation, the teacher will ask, "How smoothly do you think a large group can deal with day-to-day issues? What if each individual in the school had a say in every daily decision about running the school?" Students will probably decide that using proportional representation makes sense when larger numbers of "citizens" are involved. The teacher and students will then do some sample calculations for a house of representatives for their school. If the school serves 150 students, the class may decide that the legislature will consist of 15 representatives. The teacher will give the students information similar to that shown in Figure 5.4 and ask them to fill in the missing numbers.

Teacher	Number of Students in Class	Number of Representatives
Mr. Williams	30	
Ms. Burke	30	
Ms. Fogarty	20	
Mr. Bellanca	20	
Ms. Ward	30	
Ms. Schumer	20	

Figure 5.4

Brainstorming Principles, Beliefs, and Rules

Whether a constitution is written or informal, it is a compact that is grounded in the principles and beliefs of the social organization it serves. The teacher will explain this idea to the students and give examples of the principles that the writers of the U.S. Constitution wanted to embed in the federal constitution: individual dignity, liberty, justice, fairness, equity, and the rule of law.

The teacher then will ask students to individually develop a list of four or five personal beliefs they would like to use as the foundation of the classroom constitution. The teacher will encourage students to discuss this at home so that family or household members are aware of what the class is doing and have a chance to discuss their beliefs with the students. As the class develops a list of principles and beliefs, students will produce a poster of these principles and beliefs for permanent classroom display (see Figure 5.5).

Our Classroom Principles

- We believe we all have equal rights in this classroom.
- We believe we all have the responsibility to help each other.
- We believe in treating each other respectfully.
- We believe in following the rules to keep our classroom working effectively.
- We believe in taking our fair turn.

Figure 5.5

Writing the Constitution

Once the members of the class have adopted their statement of beliefs, they will be ready to begin writing the classroom constitution. The teacher will divide the writing task so that each team works on a specific section or article of the constitution. Areas of responsibility could be as follows:

Team 1: The preamble and name of the social organization

Team 2: Legislative membership requirements, election of members, and powers

Team 3: Executive officer qualifications, election, and duties

Team 4: Judicial officer qualifications, election or appointment, and duties

Team 5: Powers, rights, and responsibilities of classroom teams

Team 6: Amendment procedures

Team 7: Ratification procedures

In a class with more than seven teams, the responsibilities of Teams 2, 3, 4, and 5 can be divided between two teams.

Each team will write a draft of its constitutional article, and the whole class will discuss the drafts, ask for clarification, and suggest changes. Teams will revise their sections of the classroom constitution, and the whole class will meet again to approve the refined constitutional articles. Using classroom or computer lab technology, the teacher will quickly assemble the constitution and print copies for everyone in the class. Each student will receive an additional copy to take home to share with his or her family.

Testing the Constitution

Each team will discuss the finalized constitution and vote on whether or not to accept it. If the number of teams needed to ratify the constitution votes to do so, the constitution will become the official statement of the system of government to be used in the classroom. If the constitution fails this ratification test, the teacher and class will discuss the reasons why. If the concern is about pieces that seem to be missing, the teacher could suggest that the class follow the example of the colonies in ratifying the federal constitution: adopt the present document with the understanding that teams will write amendments to fill in the missing pieces as soon as the existing document is ratified. If some teams still have concerns about the wording or clarity of separate articles, the constitution will undergo another round of revision. The teacher will encourage students to produce a constitution that is ratified as quickly as possible.

Using the Constitution

As soon as the constitution is ratified, the class will hold elections. Teams may have decided that the class as a whole will act as the legislative body, or they may have decided to have a representative legislature. If the latter is the case, each team will elect its legislative representative. The legislature will elect leaders who will facilitate its functioning and make committee assignments. (Writing teams will serve as legislative committees.) The class will elect executive leaders who will appoint, with the consent of the legislature, a supreme court. The legislature will draft classroom rules. The class will use constitutional processes to promote effective day-to-day functioning of the social organization.

At this point, the teacher will focus the students' attention on the Bill of Rights, the first ten amendments to the federal constitution, and ask, "What specific rights do we want to define for members of this classroom that are not well defined in our present constitution?" The teacher and students will brainstorm a list of rights, including such rights as those relating to physical safety, respect, courtesy, privacy, inclusion, learning, and making restitution.

Each team will draft an amendment to the constitution that focuses on one of these rights as assigned by the legislative leadership. Teams then will distribute copies of the proposed amendments and lobby for their passage. The legislative leaders may decide to have teams vote on all of the amendments on the same day, or they may schedule different ratification dates for each of the amendments. The teacher, acting as an advisor, will encourage the students to complete the amendment process in a timely manner.

Keeping a Constitutional Journal

As students complete the constitution and ratify and test the document, they will keep individual personal journals of observations and reflections. The teacher will encourage students to focus journal entries on the following:

- The key interactions they have with others in the class
- The methods they or classmates used to maintain a courteous process and reach consensus
- Their beliefs about the rights of individuals and the role of government in defending those rights
- Their insights into how the rule of law promotes effective functioning of social organizations
- Their understanding of the feedback system that societies use to develop and change their constitutions

A sample format for journal entries is shown in Figure 5.6.

THE PRESENTATION

Each team in the class will do a presentation performance for another class in the school. The presentation team will tell the audience what a constitution is, explain why this concept is important for students to learn, and focus on the process of developing a constitution. Each audience member will receive a copy of the classroom constitution with the graphic showing the feedback system that represents the ongoing evolution of a constitutional government (see Figure 5.7). The teacher will make a reproducible master of this feedback loop and make copies for teams to distribute to the audience members.

The presenting team will want to help the audience experience some of the constitution-development process by having partners brainstorm beliefs and ideals, practice the skills involved in listening to understand, or speak to persuade each

Constitutional Journal

Date:

Events and actions:

Interactions with peers:

    Agreements   Disagreements   How we reached agreement

Growth of our constitution:

How this reflects our beliefs:

Figure 5.6

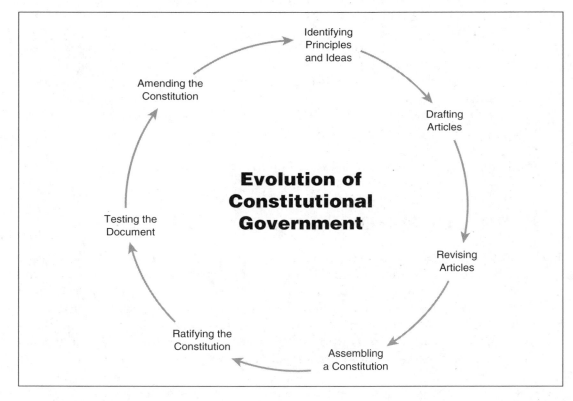

Figure 5.7

other of a point of view. At the conclusion of the presentation, the presenting team will ask audience class members to brainstorm their own conceptual definitions of what a constitution is to share with the rest of the group. This redefining activity will help the presenting team appreciate the success of its teaching.

The audience class members will write notes to the presenting team telling what they learned from the presentation performance. The presenting team will read these notes to be sure the audience class learned the information accurately. If the audience formed some misconceptions, the presenting team will write notes in reply to reinforce the correct information.

THE REFLECTION

Because this performance learning task is the only experience that most students will ever have with writing a constitution, the students and teacher will want to process and reflect to make the learning more permanent. Each student will begin by lifting his or her learning to a new level with a reflective log entry based on the acronym LIFT.

Members of constitution-writing teams will discuss their journal entries with each other, and each team will make a master list of learnings that it will share with the whole class. The class will categorize the learnings into two categories: what we learned about the concept of constitution and what we learned about the constitution-writing process. The teacher will record these learnings on a large sheet of chart paper and post it in the room for several weeks to help students remember their production of the classroom constitution.

The students and teacher will use the constitution to promote effective functioning of the classroom for the rest of the year. Whenever a procedural or rules problem arises, the teacher and students will examine the constitution and classroom rules passed by the legislature to see if the solution is suggested by the existing documents, if the class wants a new rule, or if the class wants to try to amend the constitution. This ongoing use of the classroom constitution will reinforce the concept that such a system of principles and laws constantly evolves through use, interpretation, and amendment.

Reflection

INDIVIDUAL REFLECTION
Journal Entry

L   What did I **L**earn?

I   Why is the learning **I**mportant?

F   How can I **F**ile it?
        (Memory cues? Paper trail?)

T   What will **T**ransfer? Where and how?

TEAM REFLECTION
What We Learned About Constitutions

The Concept	The Process

Cruising
the Cortex

Sightseeing for Smarts

THE AUDIENCE

Grade Level

Students of all ages can gain insight into their learning preferences by investigating Howard Gardner's (1983) multiple intelligences. Teachers can find resources to use in urban or rural setting with learners from kindergarten through college. Because this performance learning activity asks students to assemble and produce props for a "television studio" set and to understand more advanced vocabulary, it works better with students in Grades 6 and higher. Teachers can find a wealth of information about Gardner's theory and teaching to and through the multiple intelligences on the Internet.

Diverse Learners

Careful assigning of students to cooperative learning teams can result in maximum learning for all. See the Preface for suggestions about team roles and responsibilities. For this performance learning activity, the Correspondent will polish the final infomercial script, the Conductor will do the same for the visuals and commercial set, and the Dry Cell will refine the multiple intelligence activity. In larger classes, some teams will have four members, and the Conductor's role may be divided between two people. All team members will work together to brainstorm ideas for the presentation. Each teammate will participate in the final presentation of learning. By carefully matching each student to a role, the teacher can encourage feelings of relaxed alertness that lead to deeper learning (Caine et al., 2005).

Before teachers introduce this activity to students, they will look over the task development chart and the performance rubric to decide which tasks are appropriate for their grade level or for individual students. Each student will, for example, keep an individual log of ideas for the infomercial and visuals. Students may use a variety of formats in journaling, and the performance level targets for individual students will be different. Teachers will also need to adapt the activity for the developmental level of their students.

THE PERFORMANCE

Students learn how to use written language effectively and expressively by actually engaging in writing. In this performance learning task, student teams will write scripts for infomercials that teach key ideas about the eight multiple intelligences identified by Howard Gardner (1983) and emotional intelligence as described by Daniel Goleman (2006). Each infomercial will feature a definition of the intelligence, examples of how the intelligence is used in everyday life, and an audience-participation activity that immerses learners in using the intelligence.

The teacher will divide the class into nine teams and will assign one of the multiple intelligences or emotional intelligence as the focus for each team's infomercial. Each team will plan and write a script and perform the script for the rest of the class. As the team writes, each member will analyze the script for precise vocabulary choices, consistent point of view, and smooth transitions between sections.

Each writing team will present information about its intelligence to an audience, coach the audience members through the intelligence-using experience, and ask each audience member to write a reflection about how this experiential learning enriched and deepened his or her understanding of the targeted intelligence. Performance learning will occur on several levels for the writers and audience.

The team members will improve their use of written language as they write, edit, and refine the script. They will learn to identify and avoid ambiguous constructions and become more adept at using precise language to convey important ideas. Some intelligence theorists believe that the development of complex language, especially syntax, is a key factor in the development of many intelligences (Calvin, 1996). As students polish their use of language, they are strengthening the kinds of structured sequence skills involved in activities such as getting out of bed, listening to music, or selecting a brand of toothpaste. Calvin suggests that strengthening one skill that involves novel agendas and sequences may strengthen all of these skills. Both the writers and the audience will deepen their understanding of different intelligences by using each "way of knowing" in context. Because the learning is contextual and has some personal meaning, it will be stored as episodic memory and the brain will recall and use this learning effortlessly (Sylwester, 1995). Because students will be reflecting on the performance learning experience, they will create deeper neural links to the new ideas they learn (Moon, 2005).

The Prompt

If the students have no prior knowledge of the multiple intelligences and emotional intelligence, the teacher will want to introduce students to these ideas. The teacher may give working definitions of the intelligences so that students know what kinds of activities demonstrate what ways of knowing. The teacher may structure activities to introduce these intelligences to the students, or students may do intelligence inventories, and the teacher will emphasize the idea that intelligence profiles can and do change throughout our lifetimes. Students will file any intelligence inventories in their journals so that they can track their changes over the course of the school year.

One good source for intelligence inventories is Armstrong's *Multiple Intelligences in the Classroom* (2000). Students and teacher also can find many Web sites that provide intelligence inventories, score the inventories, and report the results to the person doing the exercise. A search for "multiple intelligences" or "multiple intelligences + inventories" will locate many online resources.

To set up the writing task, the teacher will ask students, "Do you know what an infomercial is? What are one or two examples of infomercials?" Students will brainstorm answers using the think-pair-share strategy: Each student will, quietly and individually, think of and write down two or three answers. Students will then pair with assigned partners to discuss their individual answers and reach consensus on one or two that they like best. Finally, the teacher will ask each pair to share its favorite answer with the rest of the class. If the class is small, each pair may be asked to share one more answer. The teacher will collect sample answers and list them where they are readily visible to all students. Next, the teacher will assign students to small working teams and explain that each team will write and present an infomercial to teach the rest of the class about one of the multiple intelligences. Students will receive their team roles, teams will do a trust-building activity, and the teacher will introduce the task.

The teacher will say that the targeted writing skills for the assignment are precise use of language, consistent point of view, and smooth, clear transitions. The teacher and students will analyze writing samples that show varying levels of skills. Students will need to know what poor use looks and sounds like, and they will need examples of excellence. Teacher and students will use a rubric to become familiar with precise descriptions of writing samples of varying levels of quality. Using the rubric will allow the teacher and each student to differentiate the curriculum by tailoring the activity to the child's level of readiness (Tomlinson, 1999).

Each team presentation will include a brief introduction of its intelligence that focuses on the intelligence's key attributes. For example, the emotional intelligence team may focus on self-awareness, managing emotions and mood, impulse control, and empathy. The bodily/kinesthetic team may emphasize physical coordination, timing, and a preference for hands-on learning. Each team will identify activities that show its intelligence in action and will give examples of typical career choices for people who are comfortable learning and working through this intelligence.

Then the team will set up an active learning experience in which audience members reinforce their learning by working in the targeted intelligence. The musical/rhythmic team could divide the audience into small teams and ask each team to rewrite a nursery rhyme so that the new poem describes the musical/rhythmic intelligence. The logical/mathematical team could have groups of audience members solve logic puzzles or play number games.

Each presentation will end with every member of the audience writing a personal definition of the targeted intelligence, giving an example of the use of this intelligence in his or her personal life, identifying one adult who he or she believes is strong in this intelligence, and explaining what the adult does that demonstrates this strength. The master script outline for all teams is shown in Figure 6.1.

Intelligence Infomercial Outline

Introduce and give a brief working definition of the intelligence.

Identify and describe the key attributes of this intelligence.

Give examples of career choices that target this intelligence.

Direct an activity to experience the intelligence.

Ask for reflections: personal definition, personal example, and adult example.

Figure 6.1

The Vision

Students may be quite familiar with infomercials. The teacher will show a video featuring several recent clips from television. Because paid programming often is scheduled for weekend mornings or late evenings, the teacher may ask the school media specialist to help in recording examples and producing an edited tape that demonstrates the key features of these infomercials: an introduction of a product or service, an explanation of what the product or service can do for members of the audience, a demonstration that may include audience participation, and testimonials about how use of the product has improved the life of someone who uses it regularly. Some programs use a hard-sell approach. Others demonstrate the product or service casually and include much friendly banter between the host and the audience.

The teacher will ask the students, "What features of these commercially used programs do you like? What do you want to use in your infomercial? How hard do you want to sell your intelligence? Do you want to do a straightforward presentation, or do you want to parody one of these salespeople?" In asking these questions, the teacher is suggesting that students carefully analyze what they see, so they can have fun producing a quality program. At this time, teacher and students will review the results of their analysis of writing samples. They may want to develop a T-chart such as the one shown in Figure 6.2 that lists examples of strong and weak use of the writing skill.

The Standards

Student teams will begin this performance learning task by researching their assigned intelligences. They will write and rehearse their presentations, present their infomercials to their classmates, and reflect on their presentation and learning. The tasks they will be doing and the developmental levels for this performance are outlined in the task development chart (see Figure 6.3).

Precise Use of Vocabulary	
Good Examples	*Poor Examples*
At least 8 out of 10	Most of them
Conclusion inconsistent with the facts	A poor idea
So excited that I began to hyperventilate	Totally happy

Figure 6.2

Teams will want their infomercials to teach correct information, engage the interest of their classmates, and help their classmates practice using the targeted intelligence. In order to do a quality presentation performance, teams will use the performance rubric (see Figure 6.4) to evaluate their infomercial during each step of preparation. The rubric will help them determine what is strong about the performance and what still needs strengthening. It can be a tool that they can use as they implement the process of *kaizen* (see Chapter 1), using its elements of teamwork, personal discipline, and suggestions for improvement (Value Based Management, 2006) in this task.

THE COACHING CONTEXT

Researching the Intelligence

As students gather information about the intelligences, the teacher can help them find helpful and age-appropriate resources. The teacher may have a classroom library with good materials on multiple intelligences and emotional intelligence, or students may search for materials in the school library. The Internet is a rich source of information on these topics. Students will be able to get their information fairly quickly with a little help and guidance from the teacher. The teacher also will have writing style manuals, samples of scripts from former student projects, and scripts from one-act plays available for students to read and analyze.

Each student will write a practice script and use the performance rubric to analyze his or her writing for the targeted skills. Students may ask for feedback from the teacher or other students as they warm up their writing muscles.

Developing the Script

As its members collect information, each team will write its own definition of the assigned intelligence and gather examples of the intelligence in action. The team will use this information to brainstorm a script for its infomercial. The Correspondent will produce a copy of the rough script for each team member, and the team will read through the script and make preliminary changes to correct the most obvious weaknesses. Each member will then do an individual revision of the rough script. The team will meet, discuss these individual versions, and draft and approve a final team

(Text continued on page 77)

Task Development Chart: Cruising the Cortex: Sightseeing for Smarts

Performance Tasks	Developmental Levels	Curriculum Standards
Meet teammates, distribute roles, receive intelligence assignment. Collect information about the assigned intelligence. Do an intelligence description. Collect ideas or suggestions for activities that target the intelligence.	**Novice** Thinks intelligence is a single, fixed brain quantity. Cannot give a working definition of intelligence. Sees no connection between experiences and learning. Is unaware of personal comfort and discomfort; thinks any problem with school is because "it's dumb, it's boring, I don't like it."	**Language Arts** Use information to form questions and support predictions. Summarize information and apply it to personal insight. Produce a script that shows clear understanding of concepts. Edit and revise for word choice, consistent point of view, and smooth transitions.
Brainstorm the infomercial script. Produce the rough draft. Select an intelligence-targeting activity. Try it out as a team; evaluate its effectiveness. Polish the script.	**Advanced Beginner** Can give a somewhat jumbled definition of intelligence. Thinks intelligence is inherited and fixed. Connects strong memories with the learning contexts. Can identify personal learning context preferences (e.g., music, quiet; at desk, on bed; alone, with a buddy).	**Fine Arts** Use elements of acting, directing, and writing to communicate with an audience. Use body, mind, voice, costumes, props, and other tools to teach the assigned intelligence.
Rehearse the script. Produce visuals, assemble props, produce audience materials. Practice the activity with buddy teams; get feedback, revise, and rehearse again.	**Competent User** Recognizes importance of experiences to learning and intelligence growth. Understands that people are smart in different ways. Knows that different people learn in different ways. Can explain and demonstrate this knowledge to others.	**Physical Development and Health** Respect peers regardless of individual differences (in intelligence comfort zones). Recognize and respect the opinions and feelings of others.
Have buddy team review the revised script. Do the dress rehearsal. Make final script adjustments.	**Proficient Performer** Recognizes importance of experience and emotion to learning and intelligence. Can name and explain different ways of being smart. Recognizes "kind of smart" targeted by different learning activities. Explains and demonstrates this knowledge to others. Tracks personal intelligence profile.	**Social Studies** Explore how personal intelligence comforts influence personal interests and perceptions. Identify ways in which cultural emphasis on some intelligences contributes to people's attitudes and perceptions.
Do the intelligence presentation. Do the activity with the whole class. Reflect on the process and the presentation performance. Do a personal intelligence profile. (Throughout the year, identify targeted intelligences for different activities. Track changes in personal profile; focus on increased comfort and strengths in intelligences.)	**Expert** Recognizes role of experience and emotion in learning and can cite research base. Can name, explain, and demonstrate different ways of being smart. Facilitates learning of others. Tracks personal intelligence profile and targets intelligences to strengthen.	**Science** Recognize that a theory is a tentative explanation of data that may change over time.

Figure 6.3

Performance Rubric: Cruising the Cortex: Sightseeing for Smarts

Developmental Level / Performance	Novice	Advanced Beginner	Competent User	Proficient Performer	Expert
Know Theories	Remembers taking an IQ test. Thinks intelligence is a fixed, single, inherited feature. Demonstrates no knowledge of history or meaning.	Has vague ideas about intelligence and "talents." Thinks intelligence is fixed and inherited. May know some names (e.g., Gardner, Goleman).	Names multiple intelligences. Believes that intelligence is a function of nurture and nature. Correctly associates researchers' names with theories.*	Names and defines emotional intelligence and multiple intelligences. Believes that intelligence follows "use it or lose it" and genetics. Has read articles and/or books about theories.	Demonstrates emotional intelligence and multiple intelligences. Explains how to strengthen multiple intelligences. Has read and can discuss original writings by Gardner and Goleman.
Apply Theories to Self	May know personal IQ as measured by Stanford-Binet IQ test. Demonstrates no knowledge of history or meaning of this score. Displays no real understanding of intelligent behavior.	Has done a multiple intelligences inventory activity. May remember highest comfort areas. Knows implications of Stanford-Binet IQ scores. Knows smart people engage in an ongoing internal dialogue.	Identifies high- and low-comfort multiple intelligences. Knows comfort can grow. Works in low-comfort area if asked to. Uses reflective or self-monitoring techniques when asked to.	Recognizes growth in comfort over time. Reflects and self-monitors without reminders. Transfers with some effort and prompting.	Describes growth in comfort with multiple intelligences and emotional intelligence. Reflects, self-monitors, and self-corrects effortlessly. Transfers automatically and easily. Targets areas of discomfort for future growth.
Demonstrate Writing Skills	Uses imprecise words. Gives a disjointed, jerky narrative. Writes with few details and/or with redundancies. Leaves several spelling and punctuation errors.	Uses generalized words and phrases: a lot, not many, "dumb idea." Uses some jumpy transitions. Gives a few supporting details. Leaves a few spelling or punctuation errors.	Uses precise vocabulary most of the time. Uses abrupt transitions. Supports and illustrates majority of main points well. Makes a few mechanical errors.	Uses precise, colorful phrasing and vocabulary. Uses abrupt transitions. Illustrates and supports most main points well. Makes no mechanical errors.	Uses Academy Award-winning script! Chooses clear, vivid vocabulary. Makes smooth transitions. Illustrates and supports all main points clearly. Makes no mechanical errors.

Figure 6.4 (*Continued*)

*AUTHOR'S NOTE: Daniel Goleman is the author of the well-known book Emotional Intelligence. This book is based on theory developed by researchers Peter Salovey of Yale University and John Mayer of New Hampshire University.

Performance Rubric: Cruising the Cortex: Sightseeing for Smarts (Continued)

Developmental Level / Performance	Novice	Advanced Beginner	Competent User	Proficient Performer	Expert
Participate in Presentation	Uses an inaudible voice. Makes no eye contact. Keeps eyes glued to the script. Shuffles feet. Coughs or clears throat every other word. Displays major stage fright.	Uses audible volume. Speaks in a monotone. Glances up from script every few minutes. Coughs only three or four times. Stands stiffly; uses no gestures. Acts scared stiff.	Uses audible voice. Uses good inflection and changes in volume. Checks place in script occasionally; maintains eye contact with audience. Uses some semirelaxed, natural gestures.	Uses good volume and inflection. Prompts teammates so they don't need to use scripts. Uses easy, natural gestures. Acts relaxed, smiles.	Uses clear, expressive voice. Ad-libs to convey the intent of the script. Prompts well and demonstrates teamwork. Acts natural, relaxed; smiles, is having fun. Puts on an Oscar-winning performance.
Facilitate Learning	Fails to communicate to audience when to participate or what to do. Displays "pour and store" behavior (expects audience to learn by listening). Lectures with no learning checks. Puts audience to sleep.	Communicates to audience when to participate but not how. Makes an attempt at interaction. Presents short bursts of "learner activity." Refers to processing but states, "We don't have time."	Repeats activity instructions only once. Leaves learners on their own to do the activity. Provides at least as much activity time as lecture. Processes quickly: what we did well.	Gives clear activity instructions. Acts as a teacher; monitors and assists learners. Majority of the presentation is activity. Processes well: what we learned, what we did well.	Reinforces instructions with overhead or flipchart. Acts as a teacher; monitors and helps as needed. Weaves activity and lecture into one piece. Processes completely: what we learned, did well, want to improve.

Figure 6.4

(Text continued from page 73)

version. The Correspondent will check this script for word choice, consistent point of view, and smooth transitions; make necessary corrections; and produce a clean copy of the script for each team member. The team will proofread the script and make any final alterations that members agree will strengthen it.

The Conductor will ask team members to brainstorm a list of props and materials the audience will need to do the intelligence-targeting activity. The whole team can decide which teammates will provide each of the various items on the list. The Conductor will produce a diagram or sketch of the set for the infomercial, and teammates will look it over and suggest changes or additions. The teacher may be able to help with some audience materials, such as paper and markers for making visuals, and the teacher will reserve a site in the classroom where each team can assemble and store its props and supplies. This site could be a large box, a section of countertop, or a shelf on a rolling cart.

The Dry Cell will select a final teaching activity to use with the audience and, with his or her teammates, will practice guiding other students through the activity.

At the beginning of the performance learning task, the teacher will announce the due date for the completed scripts. Teams may make small adjustments and changes to the script after this date, but the main script elements must be finalized by the due date.

Rehearsing the Infomercial

Once the team has a production-quality script, the Correspondent will assign each person his or her lines, making sure that the speaking parts are equally distributed among all team members. The team may want to have visuals to accompany the presentation; teammates will brainstorm the rough drafts of the visuals, and the Conductor will produce a final version to use during the presentation. Team members may decide, for example, to make a T-chart telling how their intelligence looks and sounds in action (see Figure 6.5).

Each team will assemble the necessary props, the costumes, and the materials for the intelligence-targeting activity. The teacher will assign three teams to be a practice triad so that each team can rehearse its intelligence-targeting activity with a small audience to fine-tune its facilitation of the activity. The team that developed the

---

Intrapersonal Intelligence

Looks Like	Sounds Like
Writing in a journal	I like this because . . .
Choosing to take a walk alone (to think and reflect)	I need some time to think about . . .
Using a rubric to self-evaluate	This is the strategy I used when I . . .
Putting together a portfolio to document learning	These pieces represent my learning journey best because . . .

Figure 6.5

> # Rehearsal Feedback
>
> - The intelligence we were experiencing in this activity is
> - The activity asked us to use the intelligence by
> - We felt [select one]
>
>   _____ immersed in the intelligence
>
>   _____ connected to the intelligence
>
>   _____ like viewers of the intelligence
>
>   _____ unaware of the intelligence
>
>   because _____
>
> - Our suggestions for strengthening the activity for the whole-class presentation are

Figure 6.6

activity will ask the other two teams in the triad to give feedback by responding to several statements (see Figure 6.6).

Triad teams will have at least two chances to work together before the final infomercial presentations, allowing each intelligence team the opportunity to test its activity, revise and refine it, and repeat the test run to get feedback about the effectiveness of the changes.

Scheduling the Presentations

The teacher may want different teams to present their intelligences on different days. The teacher may determine the presentation order or may have teams draw numbers to decide the presentation order. Teacher and students will discuss the presentation schedule, and the teacher will give each student a copy of the presentation schedule. The teacher and students will discuss inviting a larger audience to the presentations. This audience could include parents, other classes, or the school administrators. By enlarging the audience, the teacher and students can enhance the authenticity of the final presentations.

THE PRESENTATION

When an intelligence team takes the stage to begin its presentation, team members will begin by defining the intelligence by demonstrating some observable, intelligence-associated behaviors. The verbal/linguistic team might appear with one member reading aloud, a second writing in a journal, and a third practicing a speech. The emotional intelligence team could enter with one member saying to him- or herself, "Now just calm down. Just take a few deep breaths," and then doing this action while a second teammate says, "I'm so excited! We planned an awesome skit!" and the final team member answers, "I can see from your face that you're excited! Share the good news with me!"

Audience members will have the experience of seeing the intelligence in action, and this experiential defining creates the positive examples that glue the information to their brains. The presenting team then will give examples of finding this intelligence in the adult world: job-related tasks that use the intelligence or careers that attract people who are comfortable using the intelligence. Next, the team will guide the audience through the intelligence-targeting activity. Finally, each audience member will write a reflective journal entry that focuses on redefining the intelligence in personal terms, personal comfort or discomfort with the intelligence, and an example of how an adult in the audience member's personal life uses the intelligence positively. The presenting team will ask audience members to share their definitions and examples with the rest of the group. The teacher will conclude with suggestions about ways students could strengthen this intelligence outside of the classroom and will suggest references that contain more information about the intelligence for interested students and audience members.

THE REFLECTION

After each team completes its presentation, members will produce a visual in which they rate their performance in several categories. For each category, the team will draw an applause-o-meter and the rating that most members feel they earned. To strengthen their skills, the team will look at each of the rated categories and identify one improvement they would make in each area if they were asked to do this task again.

Finally, each team will design and produce a graphic representing an award for their performance. This award will be for their experiential learning of the targeted intelligence and the skill of writing, producing, and presenting the infomercial to "sell" their intelligence to their classmates. The teacher will encourage teams to give themselves credit for a job well done and to give themselves awards that emulate the Oscars or Emmys in style and design. This final celebration of success will solidify the positive feelings that students have about their learning and make the learning deeper and more lasting.

Reflection

TEAM REFLECTION
Rating Our Performance

Create a visual in which you rate your performance in several categories. For each category, draw an applause-o-meter and the rating the group agrees on. Then, identify one improvement you would make in each category if you were to do the task again.

Sample Applause-o-Meters

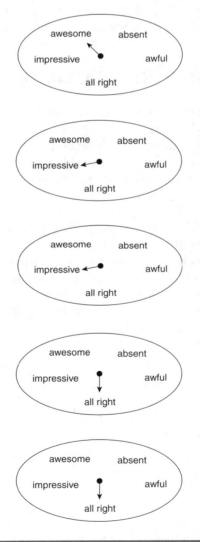

Category: Introducing and describing the intelligence

The rating we give ourselves is . . .

Our reason for this rating is . . .

One improvement is . . .

Category: Use of writing skills

The rating we give ourselves is . . .

Our reason for this rating is . . .

One improvement is . . .

Category: Giving examples of careers for the intelligence

The rating we give ourselves is . . .

Our reason for this rating is . . .

One improvement is . . .

Category: Audience-involvement experience

The rating we give ourselves is . . .

Our reason for this rating is . . .

One improvement is . . .

Category: Discussing the audience reflection

The rating we give ourselves is . . .

Our reason for this rating is . . .

One improvement is . . .

7

Patterning Neurons to Picture Patterns

THE AUDIENCE

Grade Level

Students of all ages can look for commonly repeated shapes in the everyday world. Analyzing subtle differences among similar shapes and mentally disassembling an object into its component shapes are tasks for older students, those in Grades 6 or higher. Teachers can help students find examples in urban or rural settings, indoors or out of doors. They can find a wealth of information about shapes in the natural or manufactured world by using an Internet search engine to search for "everyday geometry" and similar phrases.

Diverse Learners

Careful assigning of students to cooperative learning teams can result in maximum learning for all. See the Preface for suggestions about team roles and responsibilities. For this performance learning activity, the Correspondent will do the final scrapbook assembly, the Conductor will write the final version of the song lyrics and lead song rehearsals, and the Dry Cell will produce the final poster. All team members will participate in taking photos, analyzing them for shapes, producing "rough drafts" of the poster and song lyrics, selecting the photos to be included in the scrapbook, and presenting their information to the class. By carefully matching each student to a role, the teacher encourages feelings of relaxed alertness that lead to deeper learning (Caine et al., 2005).

Before teachers introduce this activity to students, they will look over the task development chart and the performance rubric to decide which tasks are appropriate for their grade level or for individual students. Each student will, for example, take photos and keep a personal notebook, and the performance level targets and ways of recording information for individual students will be different. Using the rubric will allow the teacher and each student to differentiate the curriculum by tailoring the activity to the child's level of readiness (Tomlinson, 1999). Teachers will also need to adapt the activity for the developmental level of their students.

THE PERFORMANCE

Students live in a world filled with natural and manufactured objects whose outlines contain a variety of geometric shapes. A well-trained eye can find rectangles, squares, rhomboids, parallelograms, triangles, circles, ovals, parabolas, hyperbolas, and more hiding throughout the everyday world. To students who do this performance learning task, these geometric names will represent more than lines drawn on a sheet of paper. These students will understand that the names represent abstractions of forms that fill the world around them, they will be able to describe the everyday world using precise language, and they will view the world with a deeper understanding of its repeating patterns. They will discover and document the fact that the world in which they live was crucial in the development of a content discipline.

Students who are learning to identify basic geometric shapes will work in groups of three to find examples of these shapes in their world and to make a photographic record of their finds. The teacher will guide students through an introduction to photographic techniques using both film and digital cameras. To demystify the production of a photographic image, the teacher will explain the basic chemical processes that occur on a strip of film and the basic electronic functioning of a digital camera.

Each student will find objects outside of school that he or she believes provide clear examples of the geometric shapes and will photograph or sketch those objects. Teammates will view each other's examples of community geometry, agree on which everyday examples show the shapes most clearly, and photograph those examples from a variety of angles. To produce a display of its examples, each team will assemble a collage containing photos illustrating each shape. Students must have an individual photo for each shape, although a photo may depict more than one shape. The teacher will arrange a gallery of these collage posters in the classroom, and all teams will take a gallery walk and study each other's collages, looking for the geometric shape or shapes in the outline of the object that is the focal point, or center of interest, of each photo.

Each team also will select a popular song or nursery rhyme and rewrite the lyrics to include the names of the geometric shapes. Students will perform the song, singing the lyrics and acting out the shapes each time they are mentioned. As students do this performance learning task, their actions will promote the formation of memory patterns for these shapes that result in deeper, more permanent, and more insightful learning. This kinesthetic learning activity promotes the formation of procedural memory patterns that, once formed, are hard to forget (Sylwester, 1995).

The Prompt

To engage students' interest in this task, the teacher will say, "Raise your hand if you know of someone who takes photos for fun or work." In many classrooms, almost every student will raise a hand. The teacher will then ask students for examples of times when these persons pull out their cameras and will suggest some examples that students may not have considered.

Students and teacher will brainstorm a list of everyday photo opportunities: parties, birthdays, holidays, family gatherings, news events, athletic contests, and celebrity sightings. Next, the teacher will ask, "What might some of these daily life photos have in common?" and record some of the answers on the chalkboard or on chart paper. These answers might include people, pets, party decorations, game playing, outdoor scenes, background views, or buildings and other structures.

Finally, the teacher will give each student a sheet showing the outlines of a variety of geometric shapes and their names and will say to the students, "How often do you think that a photo might contain one or more of these shapes? Centuries ago, people found these forms in everyday objects and defined geometric figures that are abstractions of them. You can find them in the outlines of natural and manufactured objects in your own world."

The teacher then will describe the performance learning task. Each student will find examples of objects whose outlines include at least one of the geometric shapes. Working in teams of three, students will view each other's examples, and teammates will agree on the best example to represent each shape. The teammates who found the selected examples will photograph them from a variety of angles.

Each team will obtain prints of its photos, look over the prints, choose one photo for each form that best represents it, and arrange and mount the selected photos as a collage poster. The poster will demonstrate the team's expertise in using the design elements of spacing, framing, patterning, and repetition. Other teams will analyze the collage posters, identify the basic geometric shapes best illustrated by each photo in the collage, and provide written feedback to the collages' creators. As they do this task, students will be learning some basic photography skills and embedding the basic geometric shapes of everyday life in their long-term memories.

The Vision

Collections of works by highly creative, contemporary photographers clearly demonstrate the relationship between everyday objects and geometry. As students view *Triangle, Square, Circle* by William Wegman (1995); *Shapes* by Anne Geddes (1998); or *Symmetry, Shape, and Space* by Kinsey and Moore (2006), they will see examples of these geometric connections. The teacher will help students analyze illustrations for elements of light, line, color, framing, repetition, and pattern that contribute to their overall visual appeal. Because the first two books are directed toward young children, they contain examples that are clear illustrations of the learning targeted by this performance task. These photographers demonstrate the use of natural objects in creative, whimsical ways that students may find fun and appealing. The teacher will encourage students to use these examples as models when they set up, frame, and take their own photographs.

The Standards

When teams finish this task, each member will have learned some basic photographic skills and the connections between geometry and the physical world. Each student will be able to see basic geometric shapes in everyday objects. Students may find themselves looking at an object and thinking, "Isn't that interesting? If I look at that birdfeeder from below, the roof looks like a parallelogram. Viewed from above, the roof looks rectangular." Each student will find that he or she is aware of the lighting, framing, and line of everyday scenes. Students may find themselves humming their geometry songs while they shower. The steps in the performance learning task and the curriculum standards are outlined in the task development chart (see Figure 7.1).

Students may use the performance rubric (see Figure 7.2) for this task in a variety of ways. They may compare their photos with the standards outlined in the rubric to select the examples for the collage poster. Students may self-evaluate their own skills at remembering the geometric shapes and finding real-world examples that show those shapes. A team may use the rubric to evaluate and improve its geometry song. Every student will have a copy of the rubric to use throughout the performance learning task.

THE COACHING CONTEXT

The Geometry Shapes

Students need to know what shapes to look for and identify before they begin their search for objects to photograph. The teacher will give each student a one-page guide that shows and names the basic geometric shapes (see Figure 7.3) and will suggest that students write the names and locations of the objects they want to photograph on this guide. Students can use the guide to help them keep track of the examples they identified and where these examples are located. This will facilitate the team members' work as they view the examples together, decide on the best example for each shape, and take the photos.

Photo Basics

Some students in the class may be very skilled at taking photos. Others may have never handled a camera. Teachers will poll their classes to identify the experts and the beginners before making team assignments so that they can distribute the experts among the teams in the class. The teacher also will help students find sources of information about photography. The school or classroom library may have helpful books or pamphlets. The Internet is another good source of information. A good search engine will list hundreds of sites with information about "how to take good photos."

Some students may offer the use their own cameras to their teams, and the camera owner will teach teammates how to use the camera. The teacher may provide each team with a disposable camera, purchased with budgeted funds or with funds provided by students or a parent-teacher organization, or the school may have digital cameras that students can sign out for use outside of class. The teacher and class will decide how to pay for the film processing, if needed, and printing or print-making supplies. One-use, disposable cameras can be processed at many discount stores, and these stores also print photos taken with digital cameras and sell photo paper that students can use, along with the school's computer equipment, to print their own digital photos. The students and teacher may want to ask a booster group or parent-teacher organization for help with any expenses, or the teacher may request funds for photo developing and printing from the school.

(Text continued on page 88)

Task Development Chart: Patterning Neurons to Picture Patterns

Performance Tasks	Developmental Levels	Curriculum Standards
Learn how to use a simple camera. Consider visual elements of the picture before taking it. Examine and analyze outstanding photos in class to learn these elements. Learn basic science that explains how and why film or digital electronics produces images.	**Novice** Describes shapes as straight or curvy. Holds camera upside down; cuts off tops or bottoms of objects. Uses poor lighting and no framing; shows no awareness of effective composition.	**Visual Arts** Understand the process of photography. Take photos that demonstrate an understanding of line, space, framing, repetition, pattern, and lighting. Select photographic subjects whose outlines include elements of basic geometric shapes. Arrange photos effectively in a collage.
Whole Class: Look at examples of basic geometric shapes. Review the basic geometric shapes guide. Look for examples of objects whose forms contain one of the basic geometric shapes. Look at home, in the neighborhood, anywhere but at school.	**Advanced Beginner** Confuses squares and rectangles, circles and ovals, rhomboids and parallelograms. Gets entire subject in photo with adequate lighting. Uses poor framing and composition.	**Mathematics** Identify geometric shapes contained in the outlines of everyday natural and artificial objects. Find those shapes without prompting and name them correctly.
Teams: Agree on objects to use as examples for the geometric shapes. Photograph the objects. Select the best photographs. Assemble the geometric shapes collage poster.	**Competent User** Identifies basic geometric shapes. Sees shapes in everyday objects with some prompting. Centers complete subject in photo; uses light well. Uses no other features to add pattern or perspective.	**Science** Describe how photographic media produce an image. Learn how the amount of light energy reaching the media affects the changes that result in a photographic image.
Write and rehearse the geometric shapes song. Produce copies of lyrics for classmates.	**Proficient Performer** Sees basic geometric shapes in artificial objects. Uses light and shadow, showing interesting contrast, in photo. Frames subject well; uses features to add perspective and focus interest on subject.	**Music** Demonstrate good use of rhythm by writing lyrics to a recognizable tune and naming the geometric shapes. Rehearse and deliver the song with confidence.
Do the gallery walk. Identify the shapes in other teams' photos. Point out the location of the shapes in each photo. Look at other teams' analyses of photos. Did they see what your team saw? If not, can you see what they described?	**Expert** Sees basic geometric shapes in a wide variety of artificial and natural objects. Uses lighting and color effectively in photos. Highlights subject by framing. Uses patterns to lead the eye in many directions. This person "plays with pictures."	**Applications of Learning** Connect visual analysis of objects with math. Connect math and science with the hobby of photography. Explain the connections to family members.

Figure 7.1

Performance Rubric: Patterning Neurons to Picture Patterns

Developmental Level / Performance	Novice	Advanced Beginner	Competent User	Proficient Performer	Expert
Compose Illustrative Photos	Provides no clear center of interest. "Points and shoots" without looking at photo composition. Uses too much or too little light.	Focuses center of interest so it's easy to spot. Provides no evidence of framing. Uses too little or too much light or poorly positioned light.	Provides center of interest that stands out. Uses no framing or patterning. Highlights center of interest by lighting.	Frames center of interest clearly and uses other strong images or lines. Shows well-thought-out overall composition. Uses good lighting.	Frames center of interest clearly and strongly. Adds people and/or objects to strengthen composition. Uses contrasts of light and shadow well.
Find Geometry in Everyday Objects	Does not connect abstract geometric outline with any everyday object.	Finds shapes only in artificial objects. Finds straight-line shapes but not curves. Uses correct geometry names at least 50 percent of time.	Easily sees shapes in artificial objects. Finds all shapes with equal ease. Names geometric shapes correctly at least 80 percent of time.	Sees shapes in artificial objects as a matter of habit. Uses shapes' names in discussing objects' outlines. Uses correct names all of the time.	Finds all geometric shapes in artificial and natural objects. Uses shape names in discussing outlines. Thinks in shapes in sketching objects and doing visual layouts.
Design Geometric Shapes Poster	Spaces photos poorly. Lays out photos without a plan. Leaves smudges; is messy. Omits title.	Spaces adequately. Uses grid layout. Includes blobs of paste, lots of white-out. Uses small, hard-to-read title.	Spaces adequately. Groups photos in "shape alike" clusters. Mounts and labels photos neatly. Letters title neatly.	Spaces well. Clusters photos and adds border using colored marker; nice touch. Mounts and labels photos neatly. Uses large, bold title.	Lays out photos creatively, with good spacing. Adds colorful border to each photo. Angles photos to create an overall repeating pattern. Mounts and labels cleanly. Uses eye-catching title.

Figure 7.2

Compose and Perform Song	Uses lyrics that do not match meter. Uses inaudible voice. Mumbles and mutters.	Forces lyrics to fit meter. Uses audible volume. Garbles lyrics (audience needs printed sheet to decipher them).	Fits lyrics to meter 80 percent of time. Uses good volume. Enunciates well. We could hear and follow this team.	Matches lyrics to meter well. Uses good volume. Enunciates clearly. Uses clear melody. Audience can easily follow this team.	Matches lyrics to meter and rhyme scheme well. Uses good volume, melody, and enunciation. This team is having fun! They invited audience to join in!
Produce Scrapbook and Metaphor	Uses a few photos with no shapes outlined. Does not complete metaphor.	Includes photos for 50 percent of shapes. Provides no examples of several shapes in one photo. Gives a metaphor with one "because."	Uses one photo for each basic shape. Provides no examples of a photo containing two or more shapes. Gives two "because" metaphors.	Includes at least one photo per shape, two for many. Provides one example of several shapes in one picture. Gives three "because" metaphors.	Provides at least two photos for each basic shape. Provides two or more examples of several shapes in one picture. Gives three or more "because" metaphors.

Figure 7.2

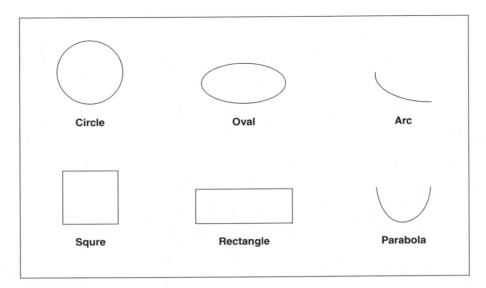

Circle   Oval   Arc

Squre   Rectangle   Parabola

Figure 7.3

(Text continued from page 84)

The teacher will want students to know some of the scientific principles that explain the production of photographic images. Teachers can find information about both film and digital image production by searching the Internet for "how photographic film works" or "how a digital camera works." A number of online sources contain sound, scientific explanations of these processes that the teacher can share with students.

Students do not need to be experts in the science of photography. The teacher will want them to know enough so that they realize that definite, explainable physical or chemical processes produce the final photographic image and print. Students and teacher will examine many examples of professionally taken photos. As they do, the teacher will point out the use of lighting and line to obtain an overall visual effect, the use of framing to focus the viewer's attention on the center of interest in the photo, the use of patterns or repetitions to suggest an ongoing process or establish a mood, and the use of a variety of camera angles to produce unique views of a subject.

The teacher will suggest that each student jot some notes about photographic techniques that he or she especially wants to remember. Books of work by noted photographers can be made available in the classroom on an ongoing basis. The teacher will encourage students to browse through these books often to refresh their memories about what they like in the techniques of these photo professionals.

The Search for Examples

Students will use their geometric shape guides to search for manufactured and natural objects whose outlines contain those shapes. Each student will begin with an individual search and keep notes of what he or she found, where the object is located, and the shape that he or she sees in the object's forms. After the teams are formed, teammates will review their notes, describe the objects to each other, share

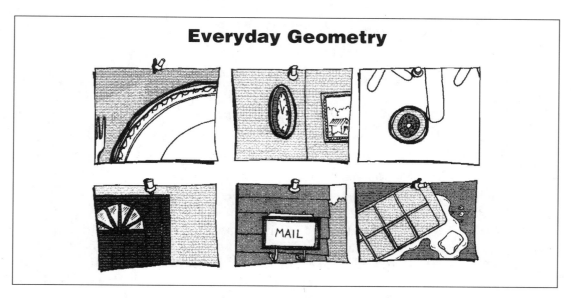

Figure 7.4

sketches or photos, and explain where the examples are located. Teammates will make arrangements to view each other's examples so that the team can agree on which object they will use to show each geometric shape. Each teammate will photograph at least two of the examples, and each object will be photographed at least twice. One-use, disposable cameras are available with film that has 24 or 36 exposures, and digital cameras store even more images, so students can take all of their photos using a single, shared camera.

The teacher and students will agree on a date by which all teams will have taken all of their photos. Students who are using film cameras will give them to the teacher, who will arrange for processing and return the finished prints to the students. Teams that are using digital cameras will be able to print their own photos using personal or school computer equipment and photo paper. Teams will examine their photos, select the best one for each object, and arrange these photos in a collage poster. Doing the collage poster will give teams another opportunity to demonstrate their understanding of the visual elements of space, framing, and patterning. Each photo will need to be bordered with a generous amount of unfilled space, because each of the other teams in the class will be placing a sticky-note comment close to each photo. Teams will title their posters, use markers to create picture-frame borders for each photo, and sign the completed work. One format for a completed collage poster is shown in Figure 7.4.

The Song

Each team also will write a song with lyrics that include the names of all the targeted geometric shapes. Teams will choose recognizable tunes, and they will practice singing their songs to be sure that the lyrics fit the rhythm. On the day of the final presentation, each team will teach its song to the rest of the class. This song is one device that will help students remember the names of the targeted geometric shapes. Following are sample lyrics, sung to the tune of "My Darling Clementine."

Geometric Shapes

Saw a circle and an oval
a hyperbola and square,
parabola and a rhombus
parallelograms to spare.
A rectangle on a corner
and an arc below a star.
Found them all and took their photos
and we noted where they are.

The teacher and class may decide that they want to publish all of the lyrics in a class "song sheet." Each student will receive a copy of these lyrics on the day of the presentation performance, and each team will take a turn demonstrating its song for the rest of the class and leading the class in song. After students hear and sing several of these songs, they will remember these geometric shapes.

THE PRESENTATION

To prepare for the presentation performance, the teacher will display the photo collage posters in the classroom, leaving a distance of several feet between posters so that each one is highlighted like a painting in a gallery. Each team will receive a small pad of sticky notes, and the teacher will say,

> When I have finished with these instructions, each team will move to its own poster, face the poster, and wait for my signal. When I say 'switch,' each team will move to the next poster on its right. The teams will discuss the photos on the poster and identify the object that is the center of interest of each photo, name the geometric figure that is contained in the outline of that center of interest, and do a small sketch of the object, highlighting the portion where they see the geometric shape in the object's outline.
>
> The teams will write this information on the *back* of a sticky note, using a separate sticky note for each photo. Each team will then write one remark on the front of the sticky note commenting on a photographic element that they think is very well demonstrated by the poster. The teams will place the sticky notes on the photos, near the bottom so that another team can still see most of the photo, making certain that the next team cannot see what is written on the back of the sticky note, and wait for another signal.
>
> When I say "switch," each team will move on to the next poster and repeat the process. When you get back to your own poster, please turn and face me. When I see all teams facing me, I will know that we are ready for more instructions.

The teacher will ask for questions, make sure that students understand the task, and direct the activity.

When teams have completed the gallery walk and are standing in front of their own posters, the teacher will say,

> Now, each team, take the sticky notes off your poster. Be sure that you know which photo goes with which group of sticky notes. Read the information on the sticky notes to see if your photo clearly showed what you intended. If another team saw something different in your photo, look closely at its sketch and the photo to see if you agree with its finding, and decide what learning you want to remember from this difference in perception. Keep track of what you and others see in each of the photos, and be ready to share that information with the rest of the class.

THE REFLECTION

Following the gallery walk and feedback review, teams will reflect on and report what they have learned about different perceptions of pictured objects. The teacher will give each team two fine-point permanent markers, one black and one blue, and will tell teams to use the black marker to outline the geometric figure(s) they saw in each photo and the blue marker to outline any other shapes other teams picked out. The teacher will provide time for teams to discuss the feedback and to outline the shapes. Then, each team will briefly explain to the class what teammates saw in their own photos, what other teams saw, and what they learned about the ways in which people perceive the same visual image. Teams will teach their songs to the rest of the class at the end of their poster reflection reports.

To transfer this new understanding about the roots of geometry to different settings, each student will search through magazines or newspapers, find new examples of the shapes in published photos, clip the photos and outline the shapes, and place the clippings in a scrapbook. The teacher will encourage the students to look for examples of objects that combine two or more of the shapes in their outlines and include these more complicated visual compositions in their scrapbooks.

Each student will also critique his or her own personal photography or visual arts skills by completing an analysis of the use of the visual elements in photography. To stretch metaphoric thinking, students will complete a sentence starter that encourages them to see geometric shapes in nature.

Reflection

INDIVIDUAL REFLECTION
How I See My Photography

Use this tool to record your self-evaluation of your picture-taking skills.

Visual Element	What's Good? How Could It Be Better?
Line and Perspective	
Framing and Space	
Lighting	
Patterning/Repetition	

When I Look at a Tree . . .

Complete the following by making at least three connections between natural objects and mathematical abstractions of their forms.

It used to be that when I looked at a tree, I saw a tree. Now I look at a tree and think, Wow! Geometry! because . . .

because . . .

because . . .

PART III

Advanced Performances

8

Half-Life in World Life

THE AUDIENCE

Grade Level

Half-life is a concept that students in Grades 7 and higher can accurately define. These students can also perform calculations involving half-life. Older students will also be able to explain the use of radioisotopes as clocks, and they can use half-life to match an isotope to a timing task. Teachers can find resources to use with urban or rural students, and applications that are meaningful for students of all socio-economic backgrounds. There is a wealth of information about "half-life," "radioactive decay," and "nuclear medicine" on the Internet.

Diverse Learners

Careful assigning of students to cooperative learning teams can result in maximum learning for all. See the Preface for suggestions about team roles and responsibilities. For this performance learning activity, the Correspondent will produce the final draft of the television newsmagazine script, the Conductor will explain calculations, collect information about the radioisotope from teammates and analyze it for bias, and check with teammates for understanding and consensus, and the Dry Cell will coach teammates on good graphing techniques and produce final versions of at least four visuals to be used during the newsmagazine presentation. Each team member will develop personal definitions of terms, prepare graphs, collect value-laden statements, and participate in the television newsmagazine report to the class. By carefully matching each student to a role, the teacher encourages feelings of relaxed alertness that lead to deeper learning (Caine et al., 2005).

Before teachers introduce this activity to students, they will look over the task development chart and the performance rubric to decide which tasks are appropriate

for their grade level or for individual students. Each student will, for example, keep a record of personal definitions, a collection of information analyzed for bias, and a log of individual insights. The performance level targets and formats for record keeping will vary for individual students. Teachers will need to adapt the activity for the developmental level of their students.

THE PERFORMANCE

Applications of nuclear science have become embedded in everyday life in many world societies. Anthropologists and archaeologists use radioactive clocks to date the remains of plants and animals and to determine the age of human artifacts. Medical professionals use radioisotopes to diagnose and treat illnesses. Nuclear medicine uses imaging techniques that show both anatomical structure and biological functioning. Irradiation is used to preserve foods by destroying bacteria, yeasts, and molds that can cause food to spoil, and irradiation is also used to sterilize packaged medical disposables such as surgical booties, gowns, masks, and gloves. Home smoke detectors contain tiny amounts of radioactive material. Students are living in a world in which uses of nuclear science are rapidly increasing. If they are to make informed, intelligent decisions about the role of nuclear science in society, they need to understand some basic concepts and realities.

A key foundational concept of nuclear science is that of half-life. Half-life is the characteristic that determines the usefulness of a radioisotope as a radioactive clock. Some applications of nuclear science require that radioisotopes have a long half-life while others require radioisotopes with short half-lives.

As students do this performance learning task, they will act out the concept of half-life, picture it graphically, read selections dealing with nuclear science uses, analyze the readings for value-laden statements, and examine public opinion toward current nuclear science applications. For the final presentation, small teams of students will deliver information about a radioisotope used in nuclear medicine to the rest of the class, and the entire class will teach another group of students about half-life by leading an experiential lesson.

The Prompt

Students may not be aware of how important the applications of nuclear science have become in medicine. The teacher will introduce this task to the students by showing them color images of brain activity associated with specific behaviors. They can find many such images on the Internet. The teacher will emphasize the fact that these pictures show the functioning of an actual person's brain as the person is engaged in a specific behavior and will ask the students, "How do you think researchers make these pictures? What techniques do they use to see brain cells at work?"

The teacher and students will review information about how cells burn glucose to get the energy they need to do work. As part of this review, the teacher will suggest that an increase in the work of cells is accompanied by an increase in the amount of glucose the cells take from the bloodstream and will say, "By tracking glucose and measuring its uptake by cells at work, we can get a picture of biological activity. We can track glucose through the body if we make the glucose radioactive." The teacher and students will then examine what radioactivity is and how half-life determines its duration.

The Vision

From the beginning of this performance learning task, the teacher and students will focus on the final presentation in which the students will report research results to their classmates and use an activity to teach another class the concept of half-life. Reports presented in television newsmagazine programs often summarize extensive research and interviewing, and students can use these productions as models for their own research reports. The teacher will show video clips of a few such reports and ask students to analyze and discuss techniques the professionals used to convey their information. A list of these techniques will include the use of photos, graphics, interview clips, and effective presentation skills.

This is a good time to introduce the concept of value-laden statements. As students watch the video clips, they will listen for statements that pack an emotional punch and record those value-laden statements. During the follow-up discussion, the teacher will ask students to share their examples with the rest of the class. As a student gives an example, he or she will identify the words that have the strongest emotional connections, describe those connections as positive or negative, and tell whether he or she believes that the values conveyed in the statement align with the realities presented in the news report.

To establish a vision of the importance of effective classroom experiences, the teacher will share a story such as, "I have a very good friend who works in medicine who struggled long and hard to comprehend the half-life concept. When I told him what we were going to be doing in class, he said, 'If I had learned about half-life the way your students will, I would have understood it from the start and felt much more comfortable with nuclear medicine as a result.' If you can understand this one concept well enough to teach it to other students, you will have a firm grasp on the foundations of nuclear science."

The Standards

Students will be learning to do a wide variety of tasks in this performance learning activity. They will learn the concept of half-life and teach it to other students, analyze the effect of biased or value-laden statements on attitudes toward nuclear science, and investigate common applications of nuclear science. The steps in the performance learning task and the curriculum standards are detailed in the task development chart (see Figure 8.1).

Students will produce and analyze graphs using half-life data, research uses of radioisotopes, use known half-lives to match radioisotopes to extended-time or short-term events and usefulness in dating artifacts, and plan and teach the concept of half-life to other students. As they work, they will want to compare their performances with the descriptions in the performance rubric (see Figure 8.2) for the task so that they can improve the quality of their demonstration of learning. Each student will receive a copy of the performance rubric early in the task. Using the rubric will allow the teacher and each student to differentiate the curriculum by tailoring the activity to each child's level of readiness (Tomlinson, 1999).

(Text continued on page 101)

Task Development Chart: Half-Life in World Life

Performance Tasks	Developmental Levels	Curriculum Standards
Do the stand/sit activity; analyze the information. Each Student: Personally define half-life and radioactive clock; explain how a radioisotope acts as a clock. Describe what happens during radioactive decay and identify alpha, beta, positron, and gamma radiation.	**Novice** "If half is gone in one half-life, the whole is gone in two!" Can't match radioactive clock to the job; wants to use a short half-life isotope to date 10,000-year-old samples or long half-life for thyroid scans. Knows that all nuclear science is bad.	**Science** Analyze and explain the atomic and nuclear structure of matter. Explain concept of half-life in own words. Explain the comment that half-life allows the use of radioisotopes as clocks. Identify some medical, food preservation, or home applications of nuclear science. Apply the half-life concept by choosing radioactive clocks with appropriate half-lives for studying short-term or extended-time events.
Do ribbon fold-cut activity and graph. Create half-life graphs using data from work with actual radioisotopes, pennies, or other materials or create half-life graphs using data provided by the teacher.	**Advanced Beginner** "If half is gone in one half-life, some is left in two, but I'm not sure how much or why." Accepts some applications of nuclear science, such as carbon-14 dating: "It's there anyway, so use it." Makes a poor match between radioactive clock and job 50 percent of time.	**Mathematics** Use half-life data to construct graphs that picture decay of radioisotopes. Use decay graphs to predict the level of radioactivity present in a sample at different times. Use ratios of activity levels to demonstrate the concept of half-life.
Do the team stand/sit activity in which each team represents a different radioisotope. Calculate the length of time required for a given number of half-lives. Pick appropriate radioactive clocks for short-term or extended-time applications.	**Competent User** Repeats memorized definition of half-life and uses it mechanically. Accepts nuclear medicine and archaeological dating; does not trust irradiation or other nuclear science applications. Picks appropriate radioactive clock for job every time.	**Language Arts** Analyze writings about applications of nuclear science for value-laden statements. Decide if a value-laden statement reflects scientific realities. Explain the concept of half-life clearly. Deliver an oral report that accurately conveys the results of research on a radioisotope.
Teams: Research the use of specific radioisotopes in nuclear medicine. Present the report to the class. Each Student: Collect and analyze value-laden statement examples.	**Proficient Performer** Applies memorized definitions and skills well. States definitions in own words with difficulty. Examines statements about applications of nuclear science for value-laden statements; analyzes the effect of those statements on personal attitudes. Picks appropriate radioactive clock for job every time.	**Social Studies** Evaluate public opinion toward uses of nuclear science. Analyze positive and negative aspects of various uses of nuclear science.
Teams: Present medical radioisotope reports to the class. Whole Class: Practice and present a half-life role play to another group of students to teach them the concept of half-life.	**Expert** Defines terms clearly and in own words; explains concepts clearly. Analyzes scientific realities and forms own opinions. Examines and explains value-laden statements made by others. Matches radioactive clocks with tasks and explains the match so others understand.	

Figure 8.1

Performance Rubric: Half-Life in World Life

Performance \ Developmental Level	Novice	Advanced Beginner	Competent User	Proficient Performer	Expert
Demonstrate Knowledge of Half-Life	Can't define or explain any terms. Thinks half-life is 12 hours of every day and radioactive clock is the snooze alarm on a bedside radio.	Recites a memorized definition of half-life. Can't explain use to time or date. Can't illustrate with an example.	Recites and explains a memorized definition. Describes clocklike attributes of radioisotopes. Applies half-life to match isotope to use.	Recites and explains a memorized definition. Describes clocklike attributes of radioisotopes. Applies half-life to match isotope to use.	Defines and explains half-life in own words and with analogies. Describes clocklike attributes of radioisotopes. Applies half-life to match isotope to use.
Graph and Calculate	Demonstrates no graphing skills: can't set up axes, plot points, draw lines, or curves. Calculates inaccurately; doesn't check answers for reasonableness.	Demonstrates weak graphing skills: axes are okay, points may be incorrectly positioned, "connect the dots." Calculates correctly 50 percent of time.	Demonstrates adequate graphing skills: good axes, positioning of points, locates straight lines well but not curves. Calculates correctly 75 percent of time.	Demonstrates strong graphing skills: good axes, point plotting, and location of "best line or curve fit." Calculates correctly almost always.	Demonstrates strong graphing skills: good axes, point plotting, location of "best line or curve fit." Uses graphs to generate new data. Calculates correctly always.
Analyze Bias in Statements	Thinks in value-laden statements without recognizing them. Doesn't allow realities to interfere with emotions. Doesn't recognize others' points of view.	Thinks in value-laden statements; knows it, believes it's okay. May not acknowledge some realities. Doesn't recognize others' points of view.	Looks for neutral ways to express information 50 percent of time. Acknowledges reality and may disagree. Argues with others' points of view.	Chooses when to be neutral and when to use value-laden statements. Acknowledges realities and defends disagreements. Argues with others' points of view.	Chooses when to be neutral and when to use value-laden statements. Says, "I see, I think" instead of "You know, it's obvious." Explains disagreements with realities. Listens to others' points of view with empathy.

Figure 8.2 (*Continued*)

Performance Rubric: Half-Life in World Life (Continued)

Developmental Level / Performance	Novice	Advanced Beginner	Competent User	Proficient Performer	Expert
Produce Newsmagazine	Uses single presenter. Acts like a "talking head." Omits graphics and role play. Can't expand on script to answer questions.	Uses single narrator. Presents one poster or transparency. Omits role play. Repeats former statements to answer questions.	Alternates narrator with other "reporters." Uses several posters or transparencies. Provides additional facts in answers to questions.	Narrates by panel. Uses several posters or transparencies. Answers questions by giving new information and making connections.	Alternates narrator with role play and panel. Uses several posters and transparencies. Answers questions by making connections to other applications.
Participate in Teaching Demonstration	Lectures for entire time. Conveys message of "read the book!"	Lectures and demonstrates. Demonstrates "see and hear." Conveys message of "I'll read the book to you."	Lectures, demonstrates, uses think-pair-share. Demonstrates "see, hear, and discuss." Conveys message of "talk it over, tell it in your own words."	Directs activity. Demonstrates "see, hear, do, and discuss." Conveys message of "experience it, retell it."	Directs activity with switch in roles. Demonstrates "see, hear, do, discuss, and teach." Conveys message of "reorganize it, teach it."

Figure 8.2

(Text continued from page 97)

THE COACHING CONTEXT

Modeling Half-Life

The teacher will begin the introduction to half-life by asking students to stand in a large circle. The circle will be positioned near a clock with a sweep second hand. The teacher will pass a pack of number cards around the circle and say, "Each of you will take one card from the pack. On your card, there is a number. I'll explain what these numbers mean as soon as each of you has a card." The teacher will have set up the pack of cards so that half of the students in the circle get cards with a face value of one, one-fourth of the students get cards with a face value of two, one-eighth of the students get threes, and so on. In a class of twenty-four students, for example, twelve will receive a "one" card, six students will get a "two," three will get a "three," and two will get a "four."

The teacher will give these instructions:

Watch the second hand on the clock. Note where it is when I say "start." After several seconds, I will say, "Ones, sit." When you hear that signal, if you have a card with a one, sit down, and write down how many seconds passed between the start and the command, "Ones, sit." Count the number of students who are still standing and record that number.

After several more seconds, I will say, "Twos, sit." If you have a card with a two, sit, count and record the number of students still standing, and note and record the total time elapsed since I said "start." We'll continue with "threes, sit," "fours, sit," and so on until only one of you is still standing.

The teacher will answer any questions the students have about the process. Then they will do the stand/sit activity. If the teacher and students believe that the activity did not go smoothly, they will talk about what went well and what needs to be improved and repeat the process. When students and teacher are satisfied that the activity was well done and only one student is still standing, the teacher will say to that student, "I'm finished giving instructions. And you're still standing. When do you think you get to sit down? When do you think you *will* sit down?" The student will possibly answer, "When I'm tired of standing." If the student does not think of this answer, the teacher will suggest it and then say to the class, "Remember that answer. We'll want to come back to it at a later time."

Analyzing the Information

Next, the teacher will ask students to set up a chart in their class notebooks to record data (see Figure 8.3). Students who counted how many others were standing will help with the last column. Everyone in the class can help with the Elapsed Time column. With the information filled in, the chart could look like the one shown in Figure 8.4.

The teacher will continue, "Look at that information. I think we may have some kind of pattern here," and will ask students to make a new chart. He or she will tell students to calculate the interval time by using the "elapsed time" numbers from the chart, so, for example, "B to A" has an interval time of 30 seconds minus zero, which equals 30 seconds. The teacher will instruct students to reduce the "standee ratio" to the simplest whole number ratio they can find.

Reference Point	Elapsed Time (seconds)	Number of Standees
A: Start	0	24
B: Ones sit		
C: Twos sit		
D: Threes sit		
E: Fours sit		
And?		

Figure 8.3

Reference Point	Elapsed Time (seconds)	Number of Standees
A: Start	0	24
B: Ones sit	30	12
C: Twos sit	60	6
D: Threes sit	90	3
E: Fours sit	120	1
And?	"When she gets tired"	0

Figure 8.4

Interval	Interval Time (seconds)	Standee Ratio
B to A	30	12:24 = 1:2
C to B	30	6:12 = 1:2
D to C	30	3:6 = 1:2
E to D	30	1:3 = 1:3

Figure 8.5

This reduces the "B to A standee ratio" from 12:24 to 1:2. The rest of the numbers fill in as shown in Figure 8.5.

Now the teacher will say, "Look at the interval times. They are all the same. Now look at the ratios. Except for the last one, they are all the same. At the end of every 30 seconds, the number of standees is one-half as great as it was at the beginning of each 30-second interval. That's half-life. We have a half-life for standing of 30 seconds. Radioisotopes have a half-life for radioactivity; after one half-life, the level of radioactivity is half of what it was before. For example, if the beginning level is 24, after one half-life the level is 12. After a second half-life, what will the new radiation level be? Look at your charts!" At least one student will say, "It will be 6! The new level will be 6!"

Picturing the Concept

Next, students will work in teams of three to take another approach to this concept. After the teacher has made the team and role assignments, the teacher will give each team at least two strips of paper package-decorating ribbon of equal length. Twenty centimeters is a good starting length. The teacher will ask one member of each team to set up axes on a sheet of graph paper as shown in Figure 8.6.

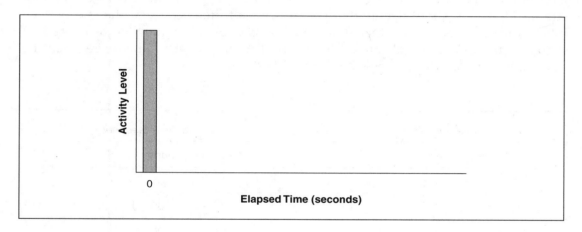

Figure 8.6

The team Dry Cell will label one strip of ribbon "A" and will tape it to the graph at time zero. The bottom end of the ribbon will touch the horizontal axis. Then the teacher will say, "Your team Conductor is your timer who will watch the clock and record the elapsed time when I say, "Fold and cut the ribbon." The team Correspondent will be the ribbon keeper. This person will fold an untaped piece of ribbon in half and will cut the ribbon at the fold when I say, "Fold and cut the ribbon." The Correspondent will hand one of the newly cut pieces to the Dry Cell to add to the graph.

The teacher's directions will continue as follows:

So here's how it will look [matching action to words]. I'll say, "Tape A to the graph," and the Dry Cell will do that. Conductors, start watching the time when you hear me say "Tape." Next I'll say, "Fold and cut the ribbon." The Correspondent will do it and will hand one piece to the Dry Cell who will label it "B." Conductors, you will record the elapsed time. Some seconds later, I'll say, "Fold and cut the ribbon." The Correspondent will do that, the Dry Cell will take the piece from the Correspondent and label it "C," and the Conductor will record the elapsed time.

We'll do the whole process two more times, so that your teams have ribbons labeled A [already taped in place], B, C, D, and E. Each Conductor will keep track of the elapsed time in a chart like this one. Time zero is the time that you tape one strip of ribbon to the graph. A is that strip of ribbon. B is the first cut-fold piece, C is the piece from the second prompt, and so on. Conductors, remember, you want to record total, elapsed time starting with my "tape" command [see Figure 8.7].

Let's do a dry run to smooth out any problems. Let me know when you get confused.

The teacher and students will practice the moves without cutting the ribbon. When the students believe that the instructions are clear, they will do the exercise, cutting the ribbon.

The teacher will ask the Correspondent and Dry Cell to work together to decide on a time scale for the horizontal axis and to tape the strips of ribbon to the graph. The ribbon graph will look like the one shown in Figure 8.8.

The teacher will ask the students, "What are we showing in this graph? What do we call the time interval between reference points? Is this another half-life demonstration?" Students will decide that yes, this is half-life because at the end of each interval the strip of ribbon that was cut off was one-half as long as the preceding strip and the time intervals are all the same. The graph shows the decrease in the radioactivity of a radioisotope—it is a half-life graph.

Reference Point	Elapsed Time (seconds)
A	none
B	30
C	60
D	90
E	120

Figure 8.7

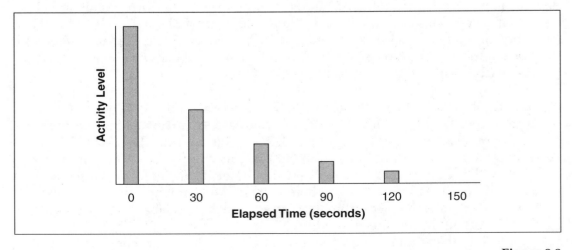

Figure 8.8

To complete the exercise, the teacher will ask students to complete the graph by drawing the straight line or smooth curve that is the best fit to the points (the tops of the ribbons). The teacher will also ask students to use the graph to generate new data. He or she may ask for the activity level after 20 or 75 seconds. Students can read this information from their half-life graphs.

Depending on the available equipment and facilities, students will next do an exercise to collect and analyze data from an actual radioisotope, or they will do another simulation. Several such simulations are found in chemistry texts such as the American Chemical Society's *Chemcom: Chemistry in the Community* (2006).

Comparing Half-Lives of Radioisotopes

Teacher and students will work with using half-life to predict how much radioactivity remains for a given radioisotope at the end of different half-life periods. The teacher will model a new exercise by standing sixteen tall objects on a desk and saying, "Suppose these represent the activity level in a radioisotope. If the half-life is ten seconds, how many objects will show the activity level after the first ten-second interval?" All of the students will probably be able to give the answer—at the end of one half-life, the activity will be one-half of its starting level—so the teacher will remove eight objects and have eight still standing.

The teacher then will say, "Now this is where things might get tricky. How many objects will show the activity level at the end of the next ten seconds?" Students will have some time to figure out the answer, and the teacher will encourage them to discuss their thinking with each other. Students will agree, after they have a chance to think, that the answer is four. They need a value that is one-half of the activity level at the beginning of that interval. The number of objects standing on the desk then will go from eight to four and then from two to one, and the teacher will say,

Now, how long will this last object represent the activity level of this radioisotope? Until it gets tired!—just as the last atom remains until its nuclear forces get tired and it gives out the last bit of activity.

Now it's time for you to figure out one on your own. I will divide the class into five teams. Each team will assume the identity of an assigned radioisotope. We will use a time scale of one second equals one day. You will start with a radioactivity level of sixteen. Your job, as a team, is to decide how much time your radioisotope will need to reach a radioactivity level of one. How many half-lives is that?

Several students will probably answer, "That's four half-lives." The teacher will thank them for the correct answer and assign each team a radioisotope. (See Figure 8.9 for examples.)

Each team will calculate the time that its isotope will need to go through four half-lives. The teacher will check the calculations for accuracy and may ask teams that have incorrect answers to double-check their calculations or explain how they got their answers. The teacher will not reveal a correct answer to any team. He or she will coach and guide, letting teams determine the correct answers.

When all teams have done the calculations correctly, the teacher will say, "Everyone, please stand up. When I say start, begin timing. Remember, we're using

Radioisotope	Half-Life (days)
Cobalt-48	71
Iron-59	46
Chromium-51	28
Strontium-85	64
Gold-198	3

Figure 8.9

a time scale of one second equals one day. When your radioisotope has reached that last atom, sit down. Watch who is standing and who is sitting. Ask yourself, 'What does that tell me about half-lives?'" Teams will notice that half-lives vary from quite short to somewhat longer. The teacher will say, "We did have a variety of half-lives, yet none was really long. What if a team had been assigned carbon-14 with a half-life of 5,770 years? That's 565,750 days! How long would that team be standing if we use the one second to one day time scale? They'd be standing for about 395 days. Would we want them to be expected to stand that long? That's a very long time to stand; then again, it's a very long half-life."

The teacher can use this information to lead into a discussion of how the atomic clock represented by each isotope is used in practical applications. Radioisotopes with short half-lives are preferred in nuclear medicine if the substance is to be introduced into the patient. A short half-life means that the radioisotope's activity level in the patient will drop to almost zero fairly quickly. The very long half-life of carbon-14 makes it very useful in dating prehistoric bones or early human artifacts. The very long half-life means that significant levels of activity will exist over an extended time.

Nuclear Medicine

Each isotope team will research the uses and role of its radioisotope in nuclear medicine. Students can obtain excellent background information about radioactivity and half-life from a variety of Web sites. An Internet search for "radioisotopes in nuclear medicine" will lead students to such sources as Berkeley Lab, a pioneer in this field.

As team members collect information from print or Internet sources, they will analyze the sources for bias, positive or negative, and they will decide how the bias of a source affects their feelings about the medical use of the radioisotope. Teams will use a television newsmagazine format to report the results of their research to the class. In these reports, teams will include their conclusions about the influence of value-laden or biased statements on attitudes toward nuclear medicine.

The Teaching Activity

The teacher and students will plan an exercise to teach other students about half-life. Students may decide to revisit the stand/sit activity the teacher used to introduce them to this concept, rehearse the instructions and movements, use the activity to demonstrate half-life to another group of students, and then lead those students in doing the activity. The entire class will act together to plan and rehearse this presentation performance of their learning.

THE PRESENTATION

For its in-class presentation performance, each team will deliver a television news-magazine report to the class that conveys the results of its research on its radioisotope. The report will include information about the use of the isotope in nuclear medicine, the diseases or disorders diagnosed or treated by use of the isotope, the affected organs or body systems, how long the use of the isotope has been practiced, alternatives to using the radioisotope, and the benefits and the drawbacks of these nuclear medicine techniques.

One member of the team will narrate the isotope report, and others will role-play doctors, patients, technicians, or others involved in the nuclear medicine application. The presentation may include role-play interviews involving the narrator, a variety of nuclear medicine characters, and the "person on the street." Team members will prepare visual aids for the narrator to use. These visual aids may include posters, overhead projector transparencies, brochures or pamphlets, or PowerPoint displays. The team will report its conclusions about the effect of value-laden statements on public attitudes toward this nuclear medicine technique, and each team will be prepared to answer classmates' questions.

In addition to the in-class presentation, the entire class will select and plan an exercise to teach another group of students the half-life concept. The class may decide to use the stand/sit activity they did to model half-life or they may choose some other activity. Whatever they choose, they will fine-tune their performance with the help of the performance rubric and with advice from the teacher. The teacher will make arrangements for an audience for this portion of the presentation performance.

After the class has worked with the audience, each audience member will write a personal definition of half-life and will include an example that demonstrates the half-life concept. When the teams return to their own classroom, the teacher will give each team some of the audience's definitions. Teams will read what audience members have written and test the audience definitions against their own under-standing of half-life to evaluate the effectiveness of their teaching.

THE REFLECTION

Using the analysis of the audience definitions as supporting evidence, each team will work together to answer an adaptation of Mrs. Potter's questions (Fogarty, 2001). Each student will also compose a personal journal entry using a sentence starter. This journal entry may help students clarify their own thinking and feelings about this often controversial topic.

Reflection

TEAM REFLECTION
Mrs. Potter and Half-Life

For our presentation to another class, we were asked to

What we did well and our supporting evidence:

What we would improve next time and our supporting evidence:

The help we believe we need and where we can get it:

What we learned about teaching and learning:

INDIVIDUAL REFLECTION
Personal Journal Entry

The two colors I would choose to represent nuclear science applications are . . .

because [three reasons for choosing each color or this combination of colors]

9

The Heart-Smart Gourmet

THE AUDIENCE

Grade Level

By the time students are in seventh grade, they are ready to learn menu planning and food preparation skills, they can handle heavy cooking utensils, and they are usually willing to sample unfamiliar foods. Healthy eating is a valuable lifelong skill for all students to acquire. Teachers and students can find resources on cable or satellite television or on the Internet. Some television programs on various networks focus on healthy, heart-smart eating. Because networks change programming fairly frequently, students and teachers will want to locate specific programs using Web sites for these networks.

Diverse Learners

Careful assigning of students to cooperative learning teams can result in maximum learning for all. See the Preface for suggestions about team roles and responsibilities. For this performance learning activity, the Correspondent/Director will make the TV show cue cards and direct the on-camera performance, the Conductor/Producer will prepare the TV set for the cooking demonstration and produce the final script, and the Dry Cell/Chef will do the on-camera cooking and use food pyramid guidelines to explain how the team's menu item fits into a heart-healthy diet. Each individual will find heart-smart recipes to share with classmates and keep an activity journal, and the entire team will brainstorm the rough draft of the script. By carefully matching each student to a role, the teacher encourages feelings of relaxed alertness that lead to deeper learning (Caine et al., 2005).

1

Before teachers introduce this activity to students, they will look over the task development chart and the performance rubric to decide which tasks are appropriate for their grade level or for individual students. Each student will, for example, collect recipes, keep a personal learning journal, and help with the test cooking. Performance level targets, journaling formats, and menu analysis will differ from one individual to the next. Teachers will also need to adapt the activity for the developmental level of their students.

THE PERFORMANCE

Apprentice chefs learn their cooking skills by working in the kitchen, preparing food with the help and encouragement of cooking masters. As chefs mince, chop, measure, and blend, they create procedural memories—automatic sequences of movements and skills that are difficult to learn and hard to forget (Sylwester, 1995). Their movements become quick, efficient, and seemingly effortless. As their skills progress, they become unaware of many of the separate steps involved in the sequence of their movements. In their brains, many separate, small movements form larger memory chunks. They can tell stories, carry on conversations, or plan ahead for the next step in the process as their muscles carry out the actions needed to do a food preparation task.

Preparing food using fresh ingredients develops lifelong skills at which most students can become proficient performers. As students combine these cooking skills with heart-smart choices of ingredients, they develop the capability to maintain enjoyable, healthful diets. In this performance learning task, students will learn cooking skills frequently used in making everyday meals. As they prepare different recipes to practice the basic skills, students will collect information about heart-smart eating and plan a menu for a heart-smart buffet. Student teams will write and perform a script for a cooking show in which team members explain and demonstrate how to prepare a heart-healthy recipe. Students will celebrate their knowledge of menu planning and cooking skills by preparing and sharing a heart-healthy luncheon buffet with invited guests.

The Prompt

The teacher will introduce this performance learning task to students by telling a story about a poor cook. Many people know a story about someone who cooks so badly that he or she once put a frozen pizza in the oven without removing the packaging. Another poor cook story could involve someone who read the instruction, "Mix by hand," and plunged his or her fingers into the mixture, not realizing that the instruction really meant to stir with a spoon or fork instead of using an electric mixer. Students will laugh at these stories, perhaps knowing they could make these types of mistakes themselves.

The teacher will ask students to stand and then say, "Please sit down when the food preparation task I name represents the most complicated food preparation you have ever done: putting ice cream in a dish, opening a bag of potato chips, making toaster pastry, making toast without burning it, cooking frozen pizza, heating canned soup, preparing a cake from a mix, preparing mashed potatoes from fresh ones, making soup from fresh ingredients, making a cake from scratch."

When all the students are sitting, the teacher will tell them that each one of them will be able to do many, if not all, of the tasks that were named by the time they complete this activity. At this time, the teacher also will encourage students to begin thinking about making heart-healthy food choices. A teacher may survey the class, asking students to raise their hands if they know someone who has been diagnosed with high blood pressure, high cholesterol, irregular heartbeat, or diabetes. The teacher will suggest that heart-healthy diets can help many individuals remediate these problems and can include many enjoyable foods.

Students and teacher will discuss the final presentation for this task. The teacher will tell the students that they will be presenting cooking programs to each other and preparing an end-of-task luncheon buffet for themselves and a survey group of students from outside the class. Teams of students will write scripts for segments of a class production, "The Heart-Smart Chef," and each team will perform its cooking demonstration for the rest of the class. Each team will prepare its presentation recipe and a few other dishes for the final luncheon buffet. The student chefs will ask members of the survey group to rate buffet items, telling which items were their favorites and which they would be least likely to want to eat again.

The Vision

A number of master chefs or cooks have their own television programs. Students and teachers can find information about available programs by searching the Internet for "television cooking shows" or "television food shows." To give students examples of excellent cooking show performances, the teacher will show several video clips from a variety of cooking programs and ask students to watch how easily the chefs prepare food as they explain what they are doing. Students will notice that these camera-wise chefs are able to stay close to the script without reading every line and to ad-lib to explain the unexpected. Students also may comment on the organization of the show. Most chefs have ingredients already measured and ready to use so they can prepare several dishes in a 30-minute program. The chef and staff of the television program often write recipes and narration, including cooking tips, on large cue cards. Watching these master chefs perform for the camera will help student teams prepare quality food programs of their own.

Seeing the cooking masters work will also help students associate some cooking actions with the words used to describe them. Many recipes that chefs demonstrate involve mincing, sautéing, simmering, dicing, blending, and other specific cooking techniques. Students who are unfamiliar with cooking skills will appreciate seeing these skills demonstrated by experts before they attempt to perform them. The video clips will show students what some cooking processes look like when they are done correctly. The teacher may also want to provide samples of food prepared by experts so that students can experience the taste of good cooking. The teacher and students can pool their funds to purchase samples of expertly cooked food or the teacher can locate funding from other sources.

The Standards

In this performance learning task, students will learn how to plan heart-smart menus while they practice cooking skills. The entire class will do menu planning; students will work in teams to learn cooking skills and to write, polish, and perform cooking show scripts. Each team will prepare food for the final luncheon buffet. Curriculum standards from several areas weave together in this complex task. The standards and steps in skill development are outlined in the task development chart (see Figure 9.1).

As students practice their cooking and menu-planning skills, revise their scripts, and prepare the luncheon, they will use the performance rubric (see Figure 9.2) for the task to evaluate their performance level for each phase of the task. Students will use the rubric to decide what they are doing well and what they want to target for improvement. Remembering that the final presentation involves both the cooking show and the buffet, students will want to use the rubric to keep track of all of the components of this performance learning task. Using the rubric will allow the teacher and each student to differentiate the curriculum by tailoring the activity to the student's level of readiness (Tomlinson, 1999).

THE COACHING CONTEXT

Apprentice Chefs

As students begin this performance learning task, they will watch expert performances and practice using some basic cooking skills. The teacher will demonstrate specific techniques to show students how to do the work and to provide a live model for the final cooking show performance that students will be doing. To practice their cooking skills, students will need access to a kitchen work area. A foods lab classroom is the ideal learning environment for developing proficiency in using cooking techniques. Before students begin to learn cooking skills, the teacher will assign them to teams of three and assign roles.

As students practice their food preparation skills, the teacher will stress the need for safe, sanitary handling, storage, and service of food and will show students how to keep work areas sanitary, tell them which cleaning products are needed for thorough cleaning and sanitizing of work areas, and give tips on other areas of concern such as safe temperatures for storing cold foods or temperatures at which hot foods can be considered ready to serve. The teacher will remind students that personal hygiene habits such as hand washing and covering sneezes are an integral part of kitchen hygiene as well. Students will have many opportunities to practice food preparation skills as they do the various parts of this performance learning task.

Learning Heart-Smart Menu Planning

Information on healthy eating habits is available from many types of sources. Heart-healthy eating and menu planning are frequent topics for newspaper food columns and health segments of newsmagazine programs. Several Web sites provide information about menu planning using the food pyramid advocated by the United States Department of Agriculture. As students become better cooks, they will discover many other sources of information about heart-smart eating.

The food pyramid guide to a healthy diet, available online, is a helpful tool for students planning their heart-smart menus. The Harvard School of Public Health, KidsHealth, the United States Department of Agriculture, and many other respected organizations have Web sites where students and teachers can obtain helpful tips about menu planning and food preparation. The school or town library may contain cookbooks with menus and tips from chefs, cardiac health professionals, and professional

(Text continued on page 116)

Task Development Chart: The Heart-Smart Gourmet

Performance Tasks	Developmental Levels	Curriculum Standards
Learn food preparation skills. Watch video clips of skilled chefs in action to fit actions to descriptions. Practice cooking skills in kitchen teams. Learn safe and sanitary ways of handling, storing, preparing, and serving food and cleaning up the kitchen.	**Novice** Eats impulsively; eats whatever he or she sees first and eats fast. Doesn't know about fat grams or vitamins and doesn't care. Acts dangerously in the kitchen, especially with sharp tools! Cooks frozen pizza in the box.	**Family and Consumer Studies** Demonstrate a variety of food preparation techniques. Plan daily menus that promote wellness. Handle, prepare, serve, and store food using safe and sanitary techniques. Explain connections between diet and health. Use label information to select heart-healthy foods.
Investigate principles of heart-smart eating. Learn about the food pyramid guide for making food choices. Find heart-smart recipes for the class to test. Kitchen Teams: Prepare and sample selected recipes.	**Advanced Beginner** Considers a few options before making food choices. Goes for what's fast or convenient. Sometimes, but not often, thinks about what's in food. Makes toast and simple sandwiches, heats canned soup, and prepares frozen entrees.	**Language Arts** Write a clear, precise script for a cooking demonstration. Make appropriate, impromptu changes in the script during the performance. Keep a personal notebook of learnings and applications.
Form menu teams and get menu team assignments. Brainstorm food preparation script. Decide on cooking show roles. Test and revise scripts. Make cue cards, posters, and transparencies.	**Competent User** Uses fresh ingredients and eats "healthy" when time permits. Falls back to fast and convenient food when time is limited. Makes salads and cooks fresh meat or fish; uses fresh fruits and vegetables.	**Mathematics** Use ratio and proportion to scale recipes up or down.
Do the cooking show performances. Give positive feedback to each team. Kitchen Teams: Reflect on performance and cooking results; plan cooking improvements for the class buffet.	**Proficient Performer** Varies ingredients for an interesting diet. Makes most heart-smart choices automatically. Finds heart-smart fast food (or fast preparation) choices. Reads, interprets, and prepares most recipes easily and well.	**Visual Arts** Use visual elements of color, perspective, patterns, spacing, and color scheme to design posters and menus.
Scale up recipes to amounts needed for buffet. Request cafeteria-size cooking utensils. Set up the room; prepare the food. Serve the buffet. Collect and analyze student ratings of buffet items. Reflect on results; plan improvements for next time.	**Expert** Looks for new and different fresh ingredients when grocery shopping and chooses heart-smart items. Stocks pantry and refrigerator with heart-smart food choices. Invents own variations on traditional recipes to make them more heart-healthy. Motto: Nothing is forbidden except excess.	**Social Studies** Compare differences in diet among various world cultures. Describe the ways in which physical geography and climate affect food resources in various world regions.

Figure 9.1

Performance Rubric: The Heart-Smart Gourmet

Developmental Level / Performance	Novice	Advanced Beginner	Competent User	Proficient Performer	Expert
Use Cooking Skills	Can't identify uses of cooking utensils. Can't chop, dice, mince, blend, or toss. Burns toaster pastry. Cooks frozen pizza in the box.	Uses low-skill items well: toaster, bread maker, refrigerator. Slices well; doesn't chop or mince. Removes frozen entree from box before cooking.	Uses mixer, food processor, microwave, and oven well. Slices, chops, and minces. Follows simple recipes easily.	Uses all kitchen tools and appliances appropriately and easily. Chops, slices, blends, and mixes well. Uses multistep recipes skillfully.	Chooses the right tool for the job in the kitchen. Performs any food preparation task easily and well. Scales recipes up or down, sometimes in his or her head. Creates own recipes.
Prepare Food	Cardboard tastes better. Cardboard is easier to chew. "Give me the cardboard."	Prepares food that doesn't taste bad, just doesn't taste like much. Prepares food that is sometimes chewy or hard. "With this I won't starve."	Prepares digestible food. Prepares food that's a little bland but overall okay. Prepares easy-to-chew food. "I'd have this again."	Prepares food with good, interesting flavor. Prepares tender, flaky, crunchy food with good texture. "Give this to me again."	Prepares food with rich, full, interesting flavor. Prepares out-of-the-ordinary food. Makes food with wonderful texture: the mouth feels what the brain expects. "I really want this recipe!"
Make Heart-Smart Choices	Heart-smart: knows something about fat; knows something about fiber. That's all I know. Does it really matter?	Knows fats and meat are bad. Knows fruits and vegetables are good. Does not offer much choice or menu excitement. Boring!	Watches amounts of animal fats. Knows some vegetable oils are okay. Uses lots of fruits and veggies. Knows a little meat is okay. Knows seasonings add interest.	Watches for saturated fat. Knows olive oil is good. Knows fruits, veggies, and fish are good choices. Substitutes beans for meat for variety. Explores spices and seasonings.	Uses the food pyramid to guide menu choices. Knows fresh ingredients have more of what the body wants. Uses exercise to help diet. Motto: The only forbidden is the bad tasting or excessive.

Figure 9.2

Design Cooking Show	Creates sketchy script; omits many important details. Gives no safety and sanitary details. Couldn't prepare the dish using the script as a learning tool. Uses no visuals.	Covers the basics but not how to cover problems. Produces something edible. Provides no sanitation and safety details. Uses no visuals.	Produces the expected food. Emphasizes cooking temperatures. Creates black and white poster with recipe.	Covers the recipe, "what ifs," and how to handle food and clean up properly. Creates black and white poster with recipes plus a transparency with cooking tips.	Uses great script! Provides necessary information for troubleshooting recipe and having a safe, clean kitchen. Uses poster with recipe and color illustration, plus cooking tips transparency.
Participate in Cooking Show	Uses one chef for all the cooking. Reads the cue cards line for line. Doesn't use improvisation to cover the unexpected. Acts uncomfortable in the kitchen.	Shares the cooking with two chefs. Does not deviate from cue cards. Uses no improvisation. Acts uncomfortable in the kitchen.	Alternates chefs. Improvises to cover bloopers and blunders. Acts comfortable with mistakes. Acts mechanical in the kitchen.	Alternates chefs. Uses self-directed humor to cover blunders. Acts comfortable and confident in the kitchen.	Alternates chefs; interacts and cooperates well. Acts comfortable with and funny about blunders. Acts confident and adept in the kitchen.

Figure 9.2

(Text continued from page 112)

health organizations such as the American Heart Association (2000) and the American Diabetes Association (2004).

The entire class will use the information acquired about heart-smart menus to select dishes to prepare for the luncheon buffet. Students will read recipes carefully to identify the food preparation skills that each recipe requires. They will learn unfamiliar skills and polish the skills they have already practiced. The teacher will help students plan a buffet menu. The buffet will include appetizers containing vegetables, fruits, grains (in bread or crackers), and proteins. Several vegetable and fruit salads and a variety of entrees containing meat, fish, or beans will be accompanied by a variety of breads, rice, or pasta and several vegetable choices. Desserts will include fruit, milk or yogurt products, and carefully chosen baked items (American Heart Association, 2000). When the students and teacher have decided which recipes they want to prepare, the teacher will arrange for the purchase and distribution of all necessary ingredients.

The teacher will assign students to kitchen teams in which they will practice their cooking skills as they test recipes for dishes that could be included in the buffet. After students have had an opportunity to test at least four recipes in each category, the students and teacher will decide on the buffet menu.

Foods in Other Cultures

As students learn more about heart-smart eating, they may encounter articles or information suggesting that some cultures have heart-healthier diets than others. Students will collect information about the diets of a variety of cultures and the overall cardiac health associated with these cultures. The teacher will encourage students to explore the effects that climate and geography may have on the diet of a particular society and to explore the role of exercise in overall fitness. Students may decide they want to sample some of the heart-healthy foods used in other cultures. The teacher may make arrangements to bring samples of some of these foods into the class or may help students locate ethnic restaurants or food markets so they can explore these cuisines on their own.

Because good nutrition is so important to overall health, students can extend their studies to examine such issues as availability of food to different populations. In wealthy countries, low socioeconomic groups may not be able to afford the fresh foods that promote the healthiest eating habits. In less developed countries, natural or political forces may severely restrict access to any food at all, and widespread malnutrition with its attendant health problems can be rampant. Exploring the problems associated with food distribution could be a valuable extension of this performance learning task.

The Television Series

Small teams of students will present the cooking demonstrations. The teacher will use previously established teams of three, at least one team for each category of foods included on the buffet menu, to do the demonstrations. Each team will write a script for a cooking program demonstrating how to cook one of the buffet items. The teacher may assign a buffet item to each team, or teams may draw their recipes at random. All of the students in the class will have prepared all of the recipes, so no team will be doing unfamiliar work. The teacher will assign roles for the cooking show production: the Conductor/Producer who keeps the team focused and on task and organizes the set for the cooking demonstration, the Correspondent/Director who guides the action during the demonstration and prepares the cue cards, and the Dry Cell/Chef who does the cooking and assembles the prepared menu item. Teammates brainstorm a script and decide what cue cards and props they need for the demonstration.

Each team will walk through the performance to see how well the script works. The teams will use actual kitchen implements and utensils during the walk-through. The only part of the real cooking task that will be missing will be the food. At each step of the rehearsal, teammates will check the chef's actions against the reality of preparing the food to see if the script accurately describes the cooking process. As the teams find problems in the script, they will revise the text and test it again. The teams will check the script to be certain it includes all necessary instructions about food-handling safety. Once a team is satisfied with its script, teammates will help the Director plan the cue cards.

Planning the Luncheon

Students and teacher will decide who they want to invite to the presentation buffet. They may invite parents or school administrators. They will invite other students, and they will tell these students that they will form a survey group that will rate the buffet items and tell the chefs which items they liked best and their reasons for their choices.

The student chefs will give information about the importance of heart-smart eating to members of the survey group several days prior to the buffet luncheon, and the student chefs will ask members of the survey group to come to the buffet prepared to taste every dish on the buffet and to give honest ratings.

Student chefs will design and produce an invitation (see Figure 9.3).

Students will know how many servings of each dish the basic recipes provide. They will use ratio and proportion to scale up each recipe so they can prepare enough food to serve everyone who is invited to the luncheon buffet. The teacher will arrange funding for the buffet. A parent-teacher organization may help with food costs, or the school budget may contain funds for this type of event. As soon as the teacher and students know how many guests to expect, students will do the final calculations for each ingredient needed, and the teacher and a student committee will go to a grocery store to select and purchase the food.

Each team will be in charge of preparing the recipe it demonstrated in its cooking program. To actually prepare the food for the luncheon, students may need to borrow mixing or cooking items from the school kitchen. The teacher will make

---

You are invited to share in
a special buffet prepared by

The Heart-Smart Chefs
in the foods lab at
Julia Child School.

Friday, January 12, 2007
at 12:30 p.m.
RSVP by Monday, January 8, 2007

Figure 9.3

arrangements to borrow any necessary items well in advance of the luncheon date to ensure the availability of all of the equipment that the students need to prepare and serve the luncheon.

The students will design and make signs to label each dish on the buffet. In addition to the dish's name, students may want to list the main ingredients in a dish, tell the source of the original recipe, and identify the part of the food pyramid to which the main ingredients belong.

Students also will prepare a rating sheet that the survey group members will fill out and turn in before they leave the buffet (see Figure 9.4).

Name of Menu Item	0 Send This to the Landfill	1 Edible if Not Exciting	2 Awesome! Give Me More!	Comments
1.				
2.				
3.				
4.				
5.				
6.				

Figure 9.4

Each member of the survey group will take at least two small bites of each item on the buffet and indicate his or her opinion on the rating sheet. The entire survey group will meet before leaving the buffet luncheon, and group members will vote to determine their top three dishes.

THE PRESENTATION

Before teams perform their cooking demonstrations, the teacher and students will review the big picture for the class. The overall vision is that these programs will fit together in a series, "The Heart-Smart Kitchen." Each team will do a final script check and revision, emphasizing the ways in which its menu item contributes to a heart-healthy diet. The team may include information about fat content and type, antioxidants present in the ingredients, fiber content, and how this menu item fits into a food pyramid diet plan. When this final check and edit have been completed, each team will present its cooking program to the rest of the class.

The Conductor/Producer will set out the utensils, mixing containers, and cooking pans the team needs to prepare the food. The Correspondent/Director will take his or her place between the cooking area and the audience and will have the cue cards in order. The Dry Cell/Chef will explain how to prepare the menu item. Because the cooking process contains elements that are hard to predict, each chef will be alert and ready to describe the action with impromptu comments. At the end of each program, the chefs will give each audience member a small food sample, and the audience members will taste the food and give the team positive feedback about its cooking skills.

After they do the cooking shows, teams will make the final selection of dishes to include on the buffet. During the morning of the luncheon, the students and teacher will set tables and prepare the room for their guests. Teams will prepare their buffet items, allowing ample time for preparing fresh ingredients and cooking foods. Each team will prepare two or three different dishes for the buffet. Teams that are preparing hot foods will have the food ready to serve 20 minutes after the guests are to arrive. This will allow time for guests to mingle and chat before they eat. Students who prepared a menu item will place that food on the buffet and refill the serving dish as needed. The teacher and students will all participate in cleanup after the guests are gone, and when the cleanup is finished, the students and teacher will take time to review and analyze the surveys and reflect on what they did well and what they have learned about heart-smart eating.

THE REFLECTION

After serving the buffet, the students will take time to look over the ways in which members of the survey group rated menu items. Students will summarize information and comments about the menu items in a TNT chart (see Figure 9.5).

The teacher and students will discuss reasons why people may choose to eat in ways that are not heart-smart. Students will use the TNT chart to prepare a list of the features of a heart-smart dish that is likely to be popular with other students. The students will see how well the top three dishes fit these criteria.

As each team completes its cooking program presentation, its members will take time to reflect and process their performance by answering a series of team reflection questions.

Throughout the performance learning task, each student will keep a notebook of individual reflections and personal heart-healthy learnings and insights. Two notebook entries, one made near the beginning of the task and one near the end, will list everything the student ate during one day and will analyze how well the student's food choices align with the food pyramid suggestions. The student will compare these two entries and look for changes in personal eating choices. Students will periodically review their goals, assess progress toward those goals, and reevaluate the heart healthiness of their food choices.

T	*N*	*T*
What menu items were TASTY? **Comments**	Which menu items were NASTY? **Comments**	What does this TELL us about choosing heart-smart foods?

Figure 9.5

Reflection

TEAM REFLECTION

How did our cooking show performance demonstrate

- Our cooking skills?

- Our abilities to improvise?

- Our understanding of heart-smart eating?

What happened that was funny?

How well did we maintain our composure?

What did classmates like about our food?

What cooking skills do we want to improve before the buffet?

INDIVIDUAL REFLECTION
Final Notebook Entry

My personal top five discoveries about heart-smart food choices:

Number one discovery:

Reason for choosing this discovery:

One way my choice of foods is changing:

One future goal:

10

A Special Holiday

AttaGram Day

THE AUDIENCE

Grade Level

Students of all ages need to learn how to become wise consumers. This performance learning activity is designed to help students learn how advertising can be used to influence buying habits. Because this task requires an understanding of higher-level terms, phrases, and psychology, it is best suited to students in Grade 7 and beyond. Students and teachers can find a wealth of information about consumerism by using an Internet search engine to find "consumer behavior," "consumers and marketing," "consumers and advertising," and similar phrases.

Diverse Learners

Careful assigning of students to cooperative learning teams can result in maximum learning for all. See the Preface for suggestions about team roles and responsibilities. The *Creating a Celebration* section of this chapter recommends using six learning teams for this activity, and that may mean that each team is composed of four or more students. Teachers who want to keep teams small have the option of using more teams and assigning a specific task to two teams. This option will be discussed in greater detail later in the chapter. If the teacher decides to limit teams to three students, the Correspondent will refine the team prototypes, the Conductor will keep a record of advertising and promotion ideas, and the Dry Cell will track production and sales. By carefully matching each student to a role, the teacher encourages feelings of relaxed alertness that lead to deeper learning (Caine et al., 2005).

Before teachers introduce this activity to students, they will look over the task development chart and the performance rubric to decide which tasks are appropriate

for their grade level or for individual students. Each student will, for example, keep a record of personal prototype and marketing ideas, learnings and reflections, and a collection of print ads that have been analyzed for their attempts to create consumer demands for the advertised products. The performance level targets and formats in which records are kept by individual students will be different. Using the rubric will allow the teacher and each student to differentiate the curriculum by tailoring the activity to the child's level of readiness (Tomlinson, 1999). Teachers will also need to adapt the activity for the developmental level of their students.

THE PERFORMANCE

During the past few decades, a number of celebration days have evolved to accompany more traditional ones. On these celebration days, individuals give others messages and tokens of appreciation, congratulations, friendship, or love. These celebrations are often modeled on Valentine's Day, Mother's Day, or Father's Day, celebrations with long histories. Various enterprises, noticing the effect that these celebrations had on the sales of goods, decided that creating a special day of appreciation and friendship could be an effective marketing strategy. In the United States, people now exchange tokens of friendship and recognition on Sweetest Day, Boss's Day, Teacher Appreciation Day, Administrative Professional's Day, and other days.

As students do this performance learning task, they will form a company to produce AttaGrams, cards that students can use to express friendship and appreciation for a classmate or to recognize and congratulate a classmate for a specific achievement or honor. This card-producing company will create and promote a day of celebration—AttaGram Day, a day when students throughout the school will send each other AttaGrams they have personalized with messages of friendship, recognition for work well done, or congratulations for special achievements or honors.

The students in the production company, AttaGram, Inc., will conduct a market survey to select card designs, promote the holiday, sell and distribute the AttaGrams, and investigate the effect of nonprice factors on customer demand for a product. They will prepare and deliver a report to an audience composed of members of other classes in which they describe their business venture and its results. At the conclusion of this performance learning task, the teacher and students will brainstorm a list of popular products that have been in high demand and suggest the promotional path that might have led to the success of these products. The task will help students better understand one aspect of the free-enterprise system that exists in many developed nations.

In addition to helping students understand market economics, this task can create an improved climate for learning in the entire school. When students receive positive feedback about their performances, or when they receive encouraging words of friendship and belonging from other students or their teachers, their emotions become engaged in school in positive ways. Students see school as a place where they can be creative and take risks because people in the school like and accept them. These positive emotions result in the production of endorphins, the neurotransmitters that reduce pain and increase feelings of well-being. Sylwester (1995) says that these positive emotions drive attention, which drives memory and enhances learning. Caine et al. (2005) say that positive emotional states result in expanded learning.

Students who believe in their ability to be successful in school—those who are self-convincers who say, "Yes, I can!"—are very likely to be engaged, successful learners. These self-convincing thoughts are produced in the midbrain region that is the seat of emotions, the limbic system (Sylwester, 2005). The AttaGrams that students receive from each other will provide the kinds of positive emotional experiences that can result in increased learning for every student in the school.

The Prompt

Students may not be aware of the number of special days that receive promotion and attention. The teacher will engage their curiosity by saying, "I've been wondering—other than Valentine's Day, Mother's Day, and Father's Day, what are some special occasion days for which people might send cards or flowers or do other special things for each other? Think about this for a while. Ask your friends and family for ideas. Search the Internet for sites on appreciation days or holidays and special occasions and come to class tomorrow with some answers to share with the class."

The next day, the teacher will collect and record the ideas the students contribute. Then the teacher will ask, "Have you ever wondered about the origins of all of these special days? Who created them? Who benefits from their commercial existence?" After students have thought about the kinds of goods that are exchanged, they can develop a list of the types of companies that make and deliver these products. Then the teacher will tell students that they will be taking on the role of a company that creates a special holiday for which it produces and markets greeting cards. Students will hear that they will be doing a market survey to select card designs, promoting the holiday and selling the greeting cards, delivering the cards to the recipients, and preparing a report to stockholders in which they describe the business venture and its success. The teacher will want to ask students, "Why go to all of this work? Why not just read about Hallmark, American Greeting, or other greeting card companies?" Teacher and students will review the importance that active learning plays in developing long-term understanding.

The final presentation for this task will be the report to the stockholders, played by students from other classes in the school. The students who are a part of AttaGram, Inc., will want to brainstorm ideas about the components of a successful business presentation. Television programs and commercials depicting business presentations will help them suggest that they will need presentation charts and graphs and copies of the report for the stockholders. The students and teacher will want to review the elements of an effective oral presentation and will develop a presentation rubric such as the one shown in Figure 10.1.

Students will use the rubric to self-evaluate and polish their skills before doing the oral presentation for this performance learning task.

The Vision

Students of all ages are targeted by advertising for many kinds of products. In any classroom, most of the students will be aware of the history of a number of high-demand products. The teacher and the students will brainstorm a list of these products, and the teacher will ask the students to analyze the factors that helped

Presentation Rubric: Oral Report to the Stockholders

Developmental Level / Performance	Boring	Bland	Wow!
Voice	Mumbles, mutters, speaks in monotone.	Uses clear, good volume. Speaks in monotone.	Uses clear, good volume and expression.
Eyes	Focuses totally on notes.	Looks up from notes. Sometimes detached.	Makes contact with various audience members. Engages audience.
Demeanor	Acts stiff and stilted.	Acts stiff and nervous. Makes small self-conscious moves.	Uses relaxed, natural gestures. Acts calm.
Knowledge of Subject	Recites notes mechanically. Doesn't hear errors.	Reads from notes. Corrects reading errors. Doesn't extemporize.	Uses notes as a general guide. Catches and self-corrects mistakes.

Figure 10.1

these products become so successful. Students will work in small teams to answer these questions:

- What kinds of advertising did the products receive?
- How did the manufacturers create interest in the products?
- How did the news media, intentionally or unintentionally, contribute to the success of the products?
- What, if anything, did the manufacturer do to create consumer competition for the product?
- How successful was that manipulation?
- What nonprice and nonpromotion factors contributed to the success of the products?

Students will collect print ads for some of these products and use the questions to analyze the ways in which the ads helped in engaging consumer interest in the products.

After teams have had a chance to discuss and answer the questions, the teacher will lead a whole-class discussion of the answers. Then the small teams will take some time to address these concerns:

- How can we help our company, AttaGram, Inc., be a commercial success?
- What actions of successful, everyday-world companies can we use?
- How can we maintain our vision of success as we do this performance task?

Students and teacher will use the answers to these questions to write a vision statement and a mission statement for AttaGram, Inc., and to develop a flowchart that outlines the operations of the company and the conditions that promote the success of those operations.

The Standards

Some commercial production companies go out of business before selling a single product item. Others are wild successes. The teacher will help students understand that between these two extremes are levels of development that form a continuous spectrum of business success. Each student will have a copy of these developmental levels to use as a reminder that success in using business skills, like all other skills, builds and grows through several developmental levels. Using this task development chart (see Figure 10.2), students also will see that business success involves using mathematics, language arts, visual arts, and sociology to enhance prior knowledge of the economic system. Students will use the task development chart and the performance rubric (see Figure 10.3) for the task to keep track of their places in the commercial cycle and to self-evaluate progress toward developing a successful production and marketing company.

THE COACHING CONTEXT

Incorporation

As the teacher leads the initial brainstorming and analyzing activities, he or she also will state very clearly that the performance learning task will involve forming and running AttaGram, Inc., a company that will manufacture, market, sell, and distribute greeting cards for members of the school community—teachers, students, staff, and administration—to send to each other. The sender of a card will include a personalized message to the receiver celebrating their friendship, thanking the receiver for something kind or helpful that he or she has done for the sender, congratulating the receiver on a personal success, or saying something such as "Thanks for being here. You add something unique to the life of our school."

To formalize this commercial start-up, the teacher and students will want to fill out a form registering the name of their business with a local government agency. Many local governments have a form called "Doing Business As . . ." that can be completed and filed for a small fee. This official registration of the business will give it more reality in the eyes of the students.

The teacher and students will write the vision and mission statements of their new company. They will discuss the company's target: to create a new special celebration day, AttaGram Day, for which students, teachers, teacher aides, custodians, cooks, administrators, bus drivers, and other support staff can buy and personalize greeting AttaGrams. The shipping department of AttaGram, Inc., will ensure delivery of each card to its recipient on AttaGram Day. Small teams in the class, representing different company divisions, will prepare reports to the company stockholders. The teams will deliver these reports to students in other classes to let the stockholders know what the company does and how well it does it.

Creating a Celebration

The teacher will assign students to small teams and assign each team a specific division, or function, of the company: research, production, marketing, sales, shipping, and management. If the teacher decides to limit team size to three students, there will probably be more than six teams in the class. The teacher will decide,

(Text continued on page 129)

Task Development Chart: A Special Holiday: AttaGram Day

Performance Tasks	Developmental Levels	Curriculum Standards
Form AttaGram, Inc. Receive team assignments. Create initial advertising. Explain special holiday and product to the rest of the school.	**Novice** Does not connect demand with production decisions. Does not connect nonprice factors with demand. "Just wants stuff" without being aware of influence of marketing or advertising strategies.	**Social Studies** Explain how procedures identify goods consumers will buy. Describe how nonprice factors (e.g., changes in consumer taste) can affect demand. Analyze techniques producers use (e.g., advertising, limiting supply, gifts, rebates) to influence price and demand. Identify the origins and meanings of several special occasions or holidays recognized in the community.
Create AttaGram prototypes. Design and distribute surveys. Analyze survey results and make production decisions. Print the AttaGrams.	**Advanced Beginner** Does not know that companies survey consumers to make production decisions. Thinks price is the main factor influencing consumers. Watches ads for sales and rebate offers.	**Mathematics** Design surveys and gather data to answer questions about consumer preferences. Display survey results in pie graph. Organize sales data in a graph, and use the graph to analyze the results of promotion techniques.
Create and post new advertising. Begin sales and sorting for distribution. Chart sales. Create promotion and analyze its effect on sales.	**Competent User** Knows production is tied to demand and consumer taste. Believes price drives demand. Knows supply and demand often drive prices up or down.	**Visual Arts** Use principles of proportion, composition, and perspective to design visually appealing advertising and AttaGram cards. Use appropriate tools (computers, copy machines) to produce AttaGram cards.
Prepare report to the stockholders. Perfect and polish the report using the performance rubric. Stage the stockholders' meeting.	**Proficient Performer** Knows production is tied to demand and customer taste. Knows companies frequently survey consumers to stay informed about changing taste and demand. Is well aware of the connection between supply and demand; knows that the time to buy is when there's "too much."	**Language Arts** Use standard writing and speaking conventions to produce a stockholder report that exhibits a clear focus, sufficient elaboration and support, and overall coherence. Produce a document of reproduction quality using a computer or word processor.
Map connections to everyday-world companies and products. Analyze influences of marketing and product design on personal buying habits. Chart "sales helpers" from the all-class mind map.	**Expert** Knows customer taste and interest change frequently. Is well aware that producers may keep supplies low to increase prices. Looks for sales, rebates, and quality of product. Researches major purchases before buying.	

Figure 10.2

Performance Rubric: A Special Holiday: AttaGram Day

Developmental Level / Performance	Novice	Advanced Beginner	Competent User	Proficient Performer	Expert
Create Advertising Campaign	Uses a few small posters very early in the process. Does not use the public address system (PA) for announcements. Other students don't get it: "What the heck is AttaGram Day?"	Makes a few small posters. Makes no use of the PA. Other students don't get it: "What the heck is AttaGram Day?"	Makes a few small, early posters. Makes a few PA announcements. "Oh, THAT'S what AttaGram Day is all about!"	Makes several small and large posters. Uses PA consistently. "Let's go buy some AttaGrams!"	Makes many large posters to educate and promote sales. Uses PA frequently. Creates effective special promotion. "Let's go buy some AttaGrams!"
Make Production Decisions	Throws together some designs. Throws out the surveys. Makes the cards and just hopes they sell.	Throws together some designs. Looks at the surveys. Makes the most popular card and hopes everyone will buy it.	Brainstorms ideas; then does card designs. Looks at the surveys. Makes the two most popular cards and pushes sales.	Brainstorms ideas; then does card designs. Looks at the surveys. Makes the top three cards and pushes sales.	Brainstorms ideas; then designs cards. Reviews surveys. Makes lots of the top three cards and a few of the others and pushes sales.
Plan Shipping Strategies	Creates a nightmare! Omits presorting. Stays up all night to sort cards. Makes lots of delivery mistakes. Makes lots of angry customers.	Acts disorganized. Presorts envelopes in no particular order. Stays up late to sort delivery envelopes by homeroom. Makes some delivery mistakes. Makes some angry customers.	Organizes early and well. Presorts envelopes in alphabetical order. Sorts delivery envelopes by homeroom. Makes a few minor delivery mistakes. Makes a few happy customers.	Organizes early and well. Presorts envelopes in alphabetical order. Sorts and color-codes delivery envelopes by homeroom. Makes a few minor delivery mistakes. Makes a few happy customers.	Organizes early and well. Presorts envelopes in alphabetical order. Sorts and color-codes delivery envelopes by homeroom. Makes no delivery mistakes. Makes many happy customers.

Figure 10.3 (*Continued*)

Performance Rubric: A Special Holiday: AttaGram Day (Continued)

Developmental Level / Performance	Novice	Advanced Beginner	Competent User	Proficient Performer	Expert
Write Stockholder Report	Has no focus. Is incoherent. Presents main points unclearly or without support. Makes five or more spelling or punctuation errors. Makes five or more handwritten corrections in document.	Has unclear focus. Is inconsistent, rambles. Presents main points unclearly or without support. Makes three or four spelling or punctuation errors. Makes three or four handwritten corrections in document.	Shows clear focus. Presents main points clearly; provides some support. Makes one or two spelling or punctuation errors. Makes one or two handwritten corrections in document.	Shows clear focus. Presents main points clearly; provides some support. Makes no spelling or punctuation errors. Produces reproduction-quality document.	Shows clear focus. Presents main points clearly; provides good support. Makes no spelling or punctuation errors. Produces reproduction-quality document.
Present to Stockholders	Shows little evidence of preparation or rehearsal. Meets "boring" indicators on presentation rubric.	Acts scripted but not rehearsed. Knows topic but not presentation skills.	Acts scripted and rehearsed. Acts stiff and stilted. Uses no spontaneity or humor. Meets "bland" indicators on presentation rubric.	Acts scripted and rehearsed. Adds some use of humor. Ad-libs with some reluctance. Mixes "bland" and "wow!" rubric indicators.	Acts scripted and rehearsed. Uses humor appropriately and effectively. Appears warm and engaging. A rubric "wow!"

Figure 10.3

(Text continued from page 125)

based on the amount of work that an AttaGram division needs to do, which divisions will be represented by two teams. The shipping division, for example, is responsible for sorting the AttaGrams and delivering each card to its designated recipient. This job involves enough work to keep two or more teams busy.

Each team will design and produce an advertising poster announcing the creation of a special celebration day for the school, AttaGram Day. Each poster will announce the celebration date, provide a capsule summary of the purpose of the day, and direct students to wait and watch for further announcements.

Members of the marketing team will write short scripts for commercials announcing the celebration, and the students, with permission from the school administration, will use the public address system to make live announcements heralding AttaGram Day.

Market Research

Each team will design and produce a prototype AttaGram. The whole class will brainstorm a list of possible card formats, and each team may decide to use a variety of layouts for the prototypes: greeting card, postcard, newspaper headline, e-mail, membership card, or any other format that members of a team think would work well for an AttaGram. Each team will produce 10–12 copies of its prototype card, and teams will exchange copies of their cards.

The teacher and students will prepare a simple market-survey tool to collect information about the sales potential for the different prototype cards. The survey could say, "Here are our proposed designs for the AttaGrams. Vote for the three that you like best and return this survey to the container just inside the door of room 312" (see Figure 10.4). The teacher will use the school's photocopy equipment to reduce the prototype cards so that all of them will fit on a single page. Students will distribute the survey forms to other classrooms and ask those teachers to encourage their students to complete and return the surveys.

As surveys are returned, members of the research team will tabulate the results and inform the class of the final rankings of the prototypes.

Production and Sales

After the research team has finished tabulating the survey results and reported the results to the rest of the class, students will discuss their production options. They may decide to limit the number of AttaGram designs they produce for sale. They may decide to produce all of the designs, making a greater number of the more popular designs and fewer of the less popular ones. Or they may decide to make the same quantity of each of the designs. The teacher will lead a discussion about which strategies students believe would be used by an everyday-world company. Students will make their final production decisions and design new advertising posters (see Figure 10.5).

The teacher and the production team will arrange to have the AttaGrams printed, and teams from the company will take turns staffing the sales table during lunch periods. Salespeople will keep careful records of AttaGram sales, and at the end of each day, the sales team will tally the number of cards sold and will enter the information in a ledger and on a sales-per-day graph (see Figure 10.6).

The sales team will use this graph during the final report to the stockholders to indicate trends of buyer activity.

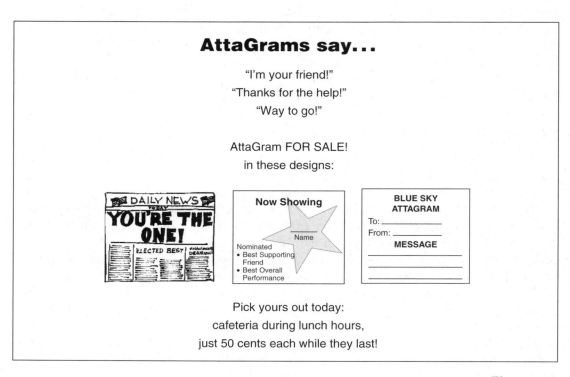

Figure 10.4

Figure 10.5

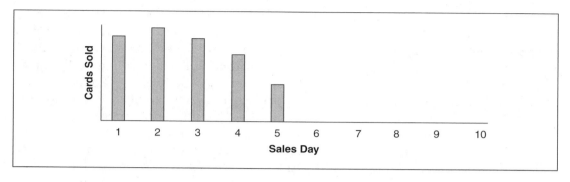

Figure 10.6

Special Promotion and Distribution

As sales begin to drop off, the students will advertise a special incentive, or promotion to increase AttaGram sales. The teacher will ask, "What kinds of incentives do everyday-world companies offer to encourage people to buy? How could you get some ideas about sales incentives or promotions used by these companies?" Students will suggest that they could watch television commercials or scan newspaper ads to collect a variety of ideas for stimulating sales. They will do the research, discuss the ideas, and make a final decision about the promotion they want to use. Students may decide to give a rebate with each sale—for example, buy an AttaGram and get 20¢ back. They may offer a gift, such as a pen, with the purchase of four or more AttaGrams. They may decide on a "buy one at full price; get one for half price" sale. Students will advertise the promotion, and the sales team will analyze the effect on sales of AttaGrams.

A few days before AttaGram Day, students will organize the greeting cards for delivery. At the end of each day of sales, students will sort and separate the AttaGrams they sold that day, putting all of the greeting cards that go to one recipient in a large envelope marked with that person's name. The shipping team will use information provided by the teacher to sort these envelopes into delivery groups. For example, if the school uses homerooms, all of the card envelopes for recipients in a given homeroom will be grouped together. When the delivery groups of AttaGrams are organized, the shipping team will give each team in the class some of the delivery bundles.

On AttaGram Day, students will take the delivery bundles of addressed envelopes to classrooms throughout the school. Students from AttaGram, Inc., will hand deliver each envelope of AttaGrams to each recipient. If a recipient is absent, the teacher in the delivery classroom will keep the envelope to give to the student when he or she returns to school. The marketing team will write a special announcement celebrating friendship and appreciation that team members will deliver over the public address system. The announcement will encourage members of the school community to give each other extra encouragement and signs of celebration throughout the day. The marketing team will want to suggest that students and teachers give each other high fives, thumbs-up signs, or other celebrations of friendship during AttaGram Day.

Report to the Stockholders

In the days that follow AttaGram Day, members of AttaGram, Inc., will prepare and deliver a report to the company stockholders. Members of other classes will play this role and will make up the audience for the presentation. The teacher will begin by asking, "What kinds of information do everyday-world companies give their stockholders? How can you get answers to this question?" Some students may suggest that family members receive booklets of information from their insurance, investment, or retirement plan companies, and offer to bring these booklets to class. The teacher and students can find Web sites that contain information that will be helpful in preparing these reports by searching the Internet for "company performance reports."

Each of the company teams will prepare its own section of the stockholders' report; make posters, charts, transparencies, or PowerPoint presentations to help in communicating the information; and prepare a copy-ready document. The teacher will arrange to have a large number of reports printed and available for members of the audience. Members of company teams will practice and polish their presentations in advance of the stockholders' meeting. Money raised by the sale of AttaGrams will be used to cover the costs of printing the reports.

THE PRESENTATION

On the day of the stockholders' meeting, AttaGram, Inc., the teams and the stockholders will assemble in the school auditorium. The teacher will make the necessary arrangements for a microphone, a presentation easel, an overhead projector, and a computer with projector. The teacher will have contacted the school's audiovisual specialist and made the necessary arrangements for having the presentation videotaped.

Each team will present its information about AttaGram Day to the stockholders. The management team will summarize the overall process, focusing on the effect of AttaGrams on the school's learning climate. The marketing team will describe how the class designed the advertising and decided on the special promotion. Members of the research team will focus on the survey to determine AttaGram design. Follow-up from the production team will focus on how the survey results determined which designs to use and how many cards of each design to produce. Using the sales-per-day graph, members of the sales team will discuss the overall trend in sales of AttaGrams and the effect of the special promotion on card sales. The shipping team will describe how cards were sorted and prepared for delivery to individual recipients. The management team will summarize the overall success of AttaGram, Inc., and provide the opportunity for audience members to ask questions. Finally, each team will summarize the main learnings of its members about the factors involved in creating a market for a new product.

THE REFLECTION

Back in the classroom after the stockholders' meeting, the teacher will say, "Let's tie what we've done to some everyday-world examples." The whole class will create a mind map for product success. The mind map, a tool for organizing information and associating ideas, was developed by Tony Buzan in the late 1960s (Buzan, 2002). Because mind maps use key words and images and are nonlinear, they reflect the way in which the human brain organizes ideas. A mind map arranges information around a strong, clear, central image that is labeled with the general theme or concept of the map. An illustrated guide to using this tool can be found online at http://www.peterussell.com/mindmaps/mindmap.html. Each team will contribute a section to the mind map in which the team names one product (or product line) that team members agree is a commercial success. To identify their focus product, teammates will sift through their collections of print ads, looking for frequently featured items. For its product, the team members will describe the targeted market group, the advertising used to promote the product, the price range, the nonprice factors that seem to influence demand for the product, and the methods used by the producer to promote sales or manipulate the market. Each team will design and produce its section of the mind map on a sheet of paper that measures approximately 15 square inches. The teacher will create the central image, How Businesses Succeed, and tape it on the wall of the classroom. The student teams will tape their sections of the mind map around this core graphic.

When the mind map is assembled, the students and teacher will examine the separate sections and then look for common threads. They may agree that price range is not necessarily a predictor of success but that target groups and marketing strategies seem to play a crucial role in commercial success or failure. The teacher and students will use a chart to summarize their findings (see Figure 10.7).

Commercial Success Helpers			
Target Group	Advertising Tactics	Promotions	Other

Figure 10.7

The class then will reflect on the overall performance learning process using de Bono's PMI (1976).

Finally, each student will write him- or herself a personal telegram. The whole-class and personal reflections will help students and teacher tie this task to everyday-world practices that they encounter every day and may help them to be more thoughtful, independent consumers.

Reflection

WHOLE-CLASS REFLECTION
AttaGram, Inc., Experience

Pluses	Minuses	Interestings

INDIVIDUAL REFLECTION
Personal Telegram

To:

Date: 10 years from now

Topic: Commercial Success

When I start marketing my own new product, I want to remember these things:

    Marketing strategies

    Nonprice influences

    Business principles

    Personal principles

PART IV

Designing Performance-Based Activities

11

Designing
Performance
Learning Activities

OVERVIEW

Creating and implementing a performance learning activity in which all students experience success requires teachers to focus on Tomlinson's (1999) three curricular elements: content, process, and product. Meticulous planning includes attention to such details as the content topics and learning standards the activity addresses, the knowledge or skills students will acquire as a result of their studies, the activities both in and out of the classroom that will scaffold students' learning, the materials that students will need to work through those activities, and the tangible products or performances that will demonstrate that students have, in fact, achieved their learning goals. Once teachers establish clear performance targets, they need to remember that the most effective strategies for reaching those goals align learning activities with assessments. Zull (2003) suggests that learning involves changes in neuronal networks in the brain, and that the two key factors leading to change are meaningful practice and valuing the learning.

Practice by itself may not lead to learning; learners must care about what they are experiencing in order for their brains to rewire themselves. McTighe (1996–97) goes farther, stating that quality learning results from ongoing, continual assessment, feedback, and adjustment, and he cites the use of this process by effective athletic coaches, music conductors, and stage production directors to support his claims.

Backward design, advocated by Wiggins and McTighe (2005), provides teachers with a model for planning performance learning activities. This lesson design process requires teachers to

- Identify desired results of the learning activity. For most classroom teachers, this means identifying the standards and benchmarks addressed by the activity;

it may also call for teachers to restate the standards or benchmarks using vocabulary that is specific to their curriculum.

- Determine acceptable evidence that students have learned, that they have met the standards. As they do this, teachers ask themselves, "How will students show that they have acquired the knowledge, skills, and attitudes that are the learning goals?"
- Plan learning experiences and instruction. When lesson planning starts with activity planning, the learning target is vague. Tomlinson (1999) calls lessons that begin with a focus on activities "hazy" and says that when teachers focus on the "what" of instruction and do not consider the "why," students do not learn what teachers expect them to. Hazy lessons do not help students understand content, and they may not even be engaging.

The Wiggins-McTighe model provides the big picture of activity design. The model outlined in Figure 11.1 fills in some of the details that teachers need to think about in planning successful performance learning activities. Sample forms for planning activities and daily logging are included in the reproducible masters section of this book.

Using Learning Teams

Many classrooms include heterogeneous learners. In such classrooms, students demonstrate differences in achievement and understanding, often represent different cultures, always possess unique profiles of multiple intelligences, may speak different first languages, may be physically disabled or challenged, and often come from very different socioeconomic backgrounds. One teacher faced with 30 or so students will have difficulty engaging all of them simultaneously. And many students, by the time they are age seven or eight, have mastered the art of looking deeply involved in a lesson when, in fact, they have tuned out.

When they are carefully structured and coached, cooperative learning teams are effective miniclassrooms that engage all learners and help them succeed. Gregory and Parry (2006) say that this practice is so successful because it immerses students in the experience of learning and permits them, within the structure of their teams, to learn in diverse ways. Sylwester's (2006b) discussion of mirror neurons suggests another reason why learning in cooperative teams results in greater success for all students. Mirror neurons activate when one person observes another performing an action or movement sequence. Because many actions or movements, like producing facial expressions or manipulating materials, are associated with information processing, and because of the interconnections among the brain's processing systems, mirror neurons may be involved in many forms of processing. The activity of mirror neurons may underlie feelings of empathy or explain the effectiveness of visualization on athletic performance.

Students who observe teammates successfully perform new skills will master those skills more rapidly, and students who hear their teammates "think out loud" as they analyze, compare and contrast, or employ other higher-order thinking skills will become more effective thinkers. When learning teams are monitored for effective use of teamwork skills, all students report that they learn communication and leadership skills that transfer into other settings.

Johnson, Johnson, and Holubec (1988) suggest that the most powerful learning teams are heterogeneous. Before assigning students to teams, the teacher needs to gather information about each individual. School records and classroom observation provide some facts, and students may be asked to provide some answers to questions about themselves. Figure 11.2 lists some fact-finding questions.

Guide to Planning
Performance Learning Activities

- Keep a personal log or journal. Use it to record plans, observations, and ongoing reflections. Using a double- or triple-entry format helps organize information.

- Look at the curricular content and ask: What topics are included?

- Ask: Why are these topics included? What standards will the study of each topic address?

- Ask: What learning do those standards suggest? What knowledge, processes, skills, and attitudes will students learn as they study a topic? How will this connect to the everyday world?

- Set up a classroom environment that supports learning for all by coaching cooperative learning skills, assigning students to heterogeneous teams, providing varied learning materials, and giving students options for demonstrating learning.

- Create the vision (the ultimate performance). Determine the evidence that shows that students have met the standards. Ask what products, performances, skills, and attitudes students need to demonstrate.

- Share the vision with students. Give them the assessment tools that they and the teacher will use. Encourage continual self-assessment; this ongoing examination of work leads to a higher-quality end result.

- If students do not understand how to use a scoring tool, show them examples of low-, medium-, and high-quality work; then ask them to compare and contrast the pieces, analyze the differences, and determine scores.

- Plan the performance learning activity. Remember to include the prompt; the coaching elements; a cycle of practice, self-evaluation, and improvement; a final performance; and a final reflection.

- Fine-tune the activity: Decide what materials or special conditions each learning task requires. Do the advance work needed to acquire materials or arrange for those special conditions.

- Lead students through the activity. Model continuous self-evaluation and improvement by having regular classroom meetings in which teacher and students analyze the effectiveness of the activity. Use ideas from students, colleagues, and personal brainstorming to fine-tune the activity.

- Facilitate the presentation, the final demonstration of learning.

- Reflect. Ask: What learning did students need to demonstrate to meet the standards? How well did they meet those standards? In this activity, what worked well? When students do it again, what will they do differently? What help is needed in revising the plan for this activity?

Figure 11.1

Fact-Finding Questions

Name:_____

- I learn best by (pick one)

     Reading/writing   Sketching/doodling   Working with objects

- I prefer to study (pick one)

     In a quiet room   With music playing

- My favorite school subject is (pick one)

     Science/math   Physical education   English

Figure 11.2

The teacher uses the background information to create teams that are as heterogeneous as possible.

Each member of a cooperative learning team has a role to perform, and each role carries with it the responsibility to do a fair share of the work of the team. General descriptions of roles for teams of three appear in the Preface of this book. Activity-specific responsibilities are described in each chapter. The teacher often assigns roles within teams to specific students, giving each student a role that aligns with a preferred or more comfortable way to learn. The teacher will give each team a set of "role cards" so that each student has a written description of his or her role. Figure 11.3 contains role cards for the roles that are used in this book, and a larger version of Figure 11.3 is included in the reproducible masters section of this book.

Role Cards

Correspondent

Checks with teammates for understanding and consensus, makes a written record of team ideas and answers to brainstorming questions, reports answers to the rest of the class.

Conductor

Keeps the team on time and on task, checks for progress toward completion of the task, does sketches or diagrams, directs rehearsals of performances or presentations.

Dry Cell

Encourages and energizes the team, uses appropriate humor to keep the task flowing, demonstrates hands-on procedures and skills.

Figure 11.3

Most of the many excellent references and how-to books that describe successful implementation of cooperative learning stress these three guidelines:

1. Small teams work better than large ones. For most classroom tasks and activities, teams of two to four students work best.

2. Teacher-assigned heterogeneous teams produce the best results. Each individual in a team brings unique strengths and skills to the group. Students who work in teacher-assigned teams learn to work with diverse partners and to look for personal strengths in all of their partners.

3. Students need to be coached in teamwork skills, and they need to be given opportunities to practice those skills. Teams need to stay together long enough to establish trust, which leads to positive interdependence and constructive working relationships. The most successful teams process their use of teamwork skills at the end of each work session and set goals for improvement. Figure 11.4 lists some suggested teamwork skills. Each time that teams work together, the teacher focuses their attention on two or three of these skills, and teams process their use of the skills at the end of each work session.

Cooperative learning, if employed thoughtfully and well, can be one of a teacher's most valuable tools in helping all students meet learning goals. Much time and planning must be put into developing a thoughtful cooperative learning activity, and the payback can be enormous.

Teamwork Skills

To work together pleasantly, politely, and "professionally":

- Get into teams quickly and quietly.

- Stay together, physically and mentally.

- Use very quiet voices.

- Take turns contributing to the flow of ideas.

- Do a fair share of the work.

- Listen for understanding.

- Use put-ups, not put-downs.

- Celebrate success together.

Figure 11.4

Topics, Standards, and Performances

In order to use this curriculum model effectively, teachers need to decide when performance-based learning is the most appropriate approach to a topic. There are other experiential approaches such as problem-based learning or project learning that may be better suited to some topics, and teachers want to remember that brains thrive on novelty (Jensen, 2005). Performance learning fits well with a topic for which

- The ideas or concepts are embedded in a particular task or performance.
- The ideas, concepts, or skills have importance in the everyday world, the world outside of school.
- The learning task is one that students will find engaging. All learners stop caring about improving their performances when a task is no longer personally meaningful to them (Caine et al., 2005).
- Specific skills that can be demonstrated for an audience are associated with learning the ideas or concepts.
- A successful demonstration of learning, showing that students really know a topic, is a requirement for moving on to the next grade or developmental level.

To decide whether or not a topic meets one or more of these criteria, teachers will want to organize their thinking about the content. Teachers will need to examine their content topics; determine alignment with national, state, and local learning standards; apply broadly worded standards to specific content; and brainstorm ways in which students can demonstrate their learning. An example of this process, using the performance learning activity from Chapter 8, Half-Life in World Life, is shown in Figure 11.5. A blank organizer for this process is included in the reproducible masters section of this book.

The Vision

Once a teacher has identified a topic as one for which performance learning is a good fit, he or she needs to create a vision, a mental model, of a high-level demonstration of learning. The teacher wants to obtain examples of expert performances to share with students. Sources of these expert pieces will vary from activity to activity. For the infomercials described in Chapter 6 or the cooking demonstrations described in Chapter 9, the teacher would want to find video segments from television programs to share with students. To explore thoughtful reading in the Chapter 4 activity, the teacher and students can examine a variety of professionally written book reviews and analyze how they demonstrate the reviewers' attention to the featured works. In finding examples, the teacher wants to connect the vision to the everyday world experienced by the students. Because cable television and the Internet tune so many students into a world beyond their neighborhoods, teachers can use these resources to find examples of excellent performances.

Topics, Standards, and Performances: Half-Life in World Life

(Chapter 8)

Topics	General Standards	Specific Standards	Performances
Nuclear change	Structure of atoms Properties and changes of properties in matter	Structure of atoms Radioactivity Changes in atoms resulting from alpha, beta, and gamma radiation Half-life	Presentation using visuals or PowerPoint showing a specific change and identifying decaying element, product element, and type of change (decay) Production and explanation of ribbon graph
Nuclear medicine	Personal and community health	Nuclear medicine	Presentation including visuals or PowerPoint, using television newsmagazine format, on a specific nuclear medicine application

Figure 11.5

Assessment Tools

As they refine the vision, teachers need to ask themselves how they and their students will assess learning. A rubric is a powerful tool that teachers and students can use for ongoing and summative assessment. Rubrics can improve student performance by making them aware, from the beginning of a unit of study, what teachers will accept as evidence that they have met learning standards (Andrade, n.d.). Using rubrics eliminates guesswork during learning and assessment. The teacher, often with help from the students, constructs the rubric before beginning the activity. Each student receives a copy of the rubric, and teacher and students inspect work of varying quality—expert, proficient performer, competent user, advanced beginner, and novice—identify the characteristics that indicate levels of proficiency, and use the rubric to score the work.

Teachers who are not experienced in creating their own rubrics can find suggestions and examples at many Web sites. Most experts agree that teachers can construct well-designed rubrics by following a few basic guidelines (see Figure 11.6).

Guidelines for Developing Rubrics

- Keep the **end in mind.** Begin with a question that doing the assessment will answer. For the television news segment, Chapter 8, one question would be, "How well does this news feature hold a viewer's attention?" For the book review people search, the question could ask, "How completely will the answers to these questions provide an understanding of the book?"

- Determine the **criteria**, the key elements or skills embedded in the performance. The most useful rubrics are short and simple; they include no more than four or five criteria.

- Determine the **indicators**, the evidence that a performance represents a particular level of learning. Many experts suggest that a useful approach is to first define an excellent performance, second to detail a bad performance, and finally to fill in the middle.

- Select indicators that describe measurable or observable elements of the performance, and make the evidence of performance internally consistent. In the rubric for Making Sense of Stories, for example, an expert performance "links characters to action with 90 percent accuracy," a competent performance "links characters to action with 75 percent accuracy," and a novice performance "can't link characters to action." The focus is internally consistent, linking characters to the action of the story. It does not shift to, for example, the relationships among the characters.

- Produce the rubric using a word processing program, and print a trial copy. The most easily used rubrics fit on a single sheet of paper.

- Test the rubric. Use it to score sample performances and products. Revise as needed.

- Use the rubric with students, ask them to evaluate it, and revise as needed.

Figure 11.6

Students who receive a rubric at the beginning of a performance learning activity and who use the rubric to continuously self-evaluate their work become better, more thoughtful judges of the quality of work that they and others produce. Teachers and students find that using rubrics demystifies grading because students know about the criteria and indicators of quality in advance of the final assessment. Using rubrics also helps teachers accommodate diverse learners. Teachers can revise definitions of acceptable evidence to set realistic learning targets for individual students, and many teachers report that routine use of rubrics results in higher-quality performances by all students. The opportunity for continuous self-evaluation and improvement results in deeper learning for all. A blank rubric form is included in the reproducible masters section of this book.

The Activity

When teachers say that they are "lesson planning," they are often talking about developing the learning activity. This is the part of the planning that focuses teachers' attention on the day-to-day classroom tasks. The activity model in this book aligns with a lesson format suggested by Madeline Hunter (1995), and it taps into practices suggested by brain research. Vital steps in the activity are the following:

1. **The Prompt:** Emotion drives attention (Sylwester, 2002). An effective prompt involves novelty with perhaps a bit of fun and mystery, and it invites students to explore learning. A prompt may be visual or verbal, and it may ask students to make predictions or to analyze unfamiliar information. In Chapter 8, the teacher asks students to analyze brain scans. Colored scans that show the brain in action engage attention, because the pictures have personal meaning to the students; the pictures show what happens in the students' own brains when they engage in those activities.

2. **The Set-Up:** During this part of the lesson, the whole class may receive direct instruction. Students often need information about the topic, so the teacher will model or demonstrate hands-on tasks and skills that are embedded in the performance learning activity. Students doing the tasks in Making Sense of Stories, Chapter 4, need to know the people search rules, and they need to receive the Three-Story Intellect and practice using its verbs. It is during the set-up that cooperative learning team members receive their role assignments. These teams need to work together for a long enough period of time to allow teammates to develop a high level of trust in each other. Throughout the unit, the teacher provides direct instruction and modeling whenever these elements are needed by the students.

3. **Guided Practice:** As teams work through the performance learning activity, the teacher monitors their work. The teacher checks with teams to see that each member is performing his or her assigned role, corrects inaccurate ideas or information, reminds teams to process their learning and use of teamwork skills at the end of each work period, and schedules time for short conferences with individuals to check on understanding and progress toward the final goals. During this time, teams and individuals use the rubric to self-evaluate the quality of their learning, and they use their self-evaluations to improve team and personal performances or to ask the teacher for additional help.

4. **The Presentation:** Teams demonstrate their learning for the teacher, another team, the entire class, or another audience. For example, after students complete their Making Sense of Stories tasks (Chapter 4), teams invite students from another class to be the audience for the final presentation. They use information from the audience to evaluate the quality and effectiveness of their performance. In Chapter 8, Half-Life in World Life, because each team has learned about a unique nuclear medicine application, classmates form the audience, and once again, feedback from the audience is used in the final self-evaluation.

5. **The Reflection**: Teams and individuals reflect on their learning in a variety of ways. Every activity in this book includes suggestions for individual and team reflection, and teachers often have favorite tools that they use with students on a regular basis. Reflection drives learning deeper and leads to transfer. Experience must be coupled with processing and reflection in order for students to apply the learning in new situations, which leads to new learning cycles (Dewey, 1938).

As teachers plan each lesson element, they need to ask themselves what activities, materials, or special conditions each element will require, and they will want to ask themselves how they can meet these needs. Careful advance planning will give a teacher the confidence needed to facilitate a successful performance learning activity.

A tool for planning performance learning activities is included in the reproducible masters section of this book.

In Conclusion

In order to be successful leaders of a performance learning activity, teachers need to believe that all students can succeed, given an encouraging classroom environment, meaningful learning tasks, and authentic self-evaluation tools. Establishing a climate in which students trust the teacher and each other is the most critical task faced by students and teacher alike. Heterogeneous, teacher-assigned cooperative learning teams need to be formed early in the school year, and students need to practice, process, and refine teamwork skills as they develop trust in the system and its stakeholders.

Teachers who are unfamiliar with this curriculum model need to keep initial performance learning activities short and simple. The activities included in this book all target several learning standards from each of four or five content areas, and a more realistic first attempt will probably target one to three standards from no more than two content areas. Starting with simple activities gives teachers the opportunity to complete a performance learning task fairly quickly, process the experience, and make the small, incremental improvements in design that lead to higher-quality activities. Developing successful performance learning activities will take teachers on the developmental path from novice to expert and help them appreciate the power of aligning learning with assessment.

Reproducibles

Task Development Chart: _____

(name of activity)

Performance Tasks	Developmental Levels	Curriculum Standards
	Novice	
	Advanced Beginner	
	Competent User	
	Proficient Performer	
	Expert	

Rubric for: _____
_____
(name of activity)

Cue: _____

Developmental Level *(Indicators)* / Performance *(Criteria)*	Novice	Advanced Beginner	Competent User	Proficient Performer	Expert

149

Performance Task Planner:
Topics, Standards, and Performances

Topics	General Standards	Specific Standards	Performances

Performance Task Planner:
Activities, Materials, and Resources

Lesson Element	Classroom Activity	Materials or Special Conditions	Sources of Help
The Prompt			
The Set-Up			
Guided Practice			
The Presentation			
The Reflection			

Performance Task Tool: Teachers' Daily Log

What was going on today?

Observations	Reflections	Ideas for Next Time

Performance Task Tool: Developmental Levels for a Performance Learning Activity

_____
(name of activity)

Developmental Level	Description
Novice	
Advanced Beginner	
Competent User	
Proficient Performer	
Expert	

PMI

P *(Pluses of the learning or my/our performance)*	M *(Minuses of the learning or my/our performance)*	I *(Interesting insights about the learning or my/our performance)*

People Search

Find someone who can respond to each of the following questions, statements, or instructions. Ask that person to speak, sketch, sing, or otherwise demonstrate the answer and to sign this sheet next to the appropriate question or statement. A person can sign only one time.

1.	2.
3.	4.
5.	6.
7.	8.
9.	10.

LIFT to Transfer
(Strengthen Those Neural Connections)

L What did I **L**earn?

I Why is the learning **I**mportant?

F How can I **F**ile it?
(Memory cues? Paper trail?)

T What will **T**ransfer? Where and how?

Role Cards

Correspondent

Checks with teammates for understanding and consensus, makes a written record of team ideas and answers to brainstorming questions, reports answers to the rest of the class.

Conductor

Keeps the team on time and on task, checks for progress toward completion of the task, does sketches or diagrams, directs rehearsals of performances or presentations.

Dry Cell

Encourages and energizes the team, uses appropriate humor to keep the task flowing, demonstrates hands-on procedures and skills.

References and Recommended Readings

Addison, K. (n.d.) *School composting*. Retrieved August 21, 2006, from http://journeytoforever.org/edu_compost.htm

American Chemical Society. (2006). *Chemcom: Chemistry in the community* (5th ed.). New York: W. H. Freeman.

American Diabetes Association. (2004). *The diabetes and heart healthy cookbook*. Alexandria, VA: American Diabetes Association.

American Heart Association (Ed.). (2000). *Low-fat & luscious desserts*. New York: Clarkson Potter.

Andrade, H. G. (n.d.). *Understanding rubrics*. Retrieved September 19, 2006, from http://www.middleweb.com

Armstrong, T. (2000). *Multiple intelligences in the classroom* (2nd ed.). Alexandria, VA: Association for Supervision and Curriculum Development.

Barro, R. (1996). *Getting it right: Markets and choices in a free society*. Boston: MIT Press.

Beers, K. (2000). *Reading skills and strategies: Reaching reluctant readers*. Elements of Literature Series: Grades 6–12. Austin, TX: Holt, Rinehart, and Winston.

Bellanca, J., & Fogarty, R. (2001). *Blueprints for achievement in the cooperative classroom*. Thousand Oaks, CA: Corwin Press.

Bowman, S. (1990). *Radiocarbon dating*. Berkeley: University of California Press.

Buzan, T. (2002). *How to mind map*. New York: HarperCollins.

Caine, R. N., & Caine, G. (1991). *Making connections: Teaching and the human brain*. Alexandria, VA: Association for Supervision and Curriculum Development.

Caine, R. N., Caine, G., McClintic, C., & Klimek, K. (2005). *12 brain/mind learning principles in action: The fieldbook for making connections, teaching, and the human brain*. Thousand Oaks, CA: Corwin Press.

Calvin, W. (1996). *How brains think: Evolving intelligence then and now*. New York: Basic Books.

Campbell, D. (1983). *Introduction to the musical brain*. St. Louis, MO: MBB Music.

Campbell, D. (1997). *The Mozart effect: Tapping the power of music to heal the body, strengthen the mind, and unlock the creative spirit*. New York: Avon Books.

Campbell, S. (1998). *Let it rot: The gardener's guide to composting*. Pownal, VT: Storey Books.

Carnig, J. (2005). Saint Paul Chamber Orchestra moves children with music program during Chicago residency [electronic version]. *University of Chicago Chronicle, 25*(5).

Cole, J. (1995). *The magic school bus gets baked in a cake*. New York: Scholastic.

Copland, A. (1988). *What to listen for in music*. New York: Mentor Books.

Costa, A. (1981). Teaching for intelligent behavior. *Educational Leadership, 39*(1), 29–32.

Costa, A. (Ed.). (2001). *Developing minds: A resource book for teaching thinking* (3rd ed.). Alexandria, VA: Association for Supervision and Curriculum Development.

Covey, S. (1989). *The seven habits of highly effective people*. New York: Simon & Schuster.

Csikszentmihalyi, M. (1990). *Flow: The psychology of optimal experience*. New York: Harper & Row.

Csikszentmihalyi, M. (2002). *Thoughts about education*. Retrieved September 14, 2006, from http://www.newhorizons.org

De Bono, E. (1976). *Teaching thinking.* New York: Penguin.

Dewey, J. (1916). *Democracy and education.* New York: Free Press.

Dewey, J. (1938). *Experience and education.* New York: Collier Books.

Diamond, M. (1988). *Enriching heredity: The impact of the environment on the anatomy of the brain.* New York: Free Press.

Eastman Kodak Staff. (1995). *How to take good pictures.* New York: Ballantine Books.

Fogarty, R. (1997). *Problem based learning and other curriculum models for the multiple intelligences classroom.* Thousand Oaks, CA: Corwin Press.

Fogarty, R. (2001). *Brain-compatible classrooms* (2nd ed.). Thousand Oaks, CA: Corwin Press.

Fogarty, R., & Opeka, K. (1988). *Start them thinking: A handbook of classroom strategies for the early years.* Thousand Oaks, CA: Corwin Press.

Francis, R. (1998). *The complete book of compost.* New York: Berkeley.

Fritz, J. (1997). *Shhh! We're writing the constitution* (reissue ed.). New York: Putnam.

Gardner, H. (1983). *Frames of mind: The theory of multiple intelligences.* New York: Basic Books.

Gardner, H. (1991). *The unschooled mind.* New York, Basic Books.

Gardner, H. (1993). *Multiple intelligences: The theory in practice.* New York: Basic Books.

Gardner, H. (2000). *Intelligence reframed: multiple intelligences for the 21st century.* New York: Basic Books.

Geddes, A. (1996). *Down in the garden.* San Rafael, CA: Cedco.

Geddes, A. (1998). *Shapes.* San Rafael, CA: Cedco.

Goleman, D. (2006). *Emotional intelligence* (10th anniversary ed.). New York: Bantam Books.

Gregory, G., & Chapman, C. (2006). *Differentiated instructional strategies: One size doesn't fit all.* Thousand Oaks, CA: Corwin Press.

Gregory, G., & Parry, T. (2006). *Designing brain-compatible learning.* Thousand Oaks, CA: Corwin Press.

Health Magazine Staff (Ed.). (2003). *Healthy heart cookbook.* Des Moines, IA: Oxmoor House.

Hunter, M. (1995). *Teach for transfer.* Thousand Oaks, CA: Corwin Press.

Jensen, E. (1995). *The learning brain.* San Diego, CA: Turning Point.

Jensen, E. (2002). *Musical arts make sense!* Retrieved September 11, 2006, from http://www.songsforteaching.com/ericjensen/2.htm

Jensen, E. (2005). *Teaching with the brain in mind.* Alexandria, VA: Association for Supervision and Curriculum Development.

Jesperson, J., & Fitz-Randolph, J. (1996). *Mummies, dinosaurs, moon rocks: How we know how old things are.* New York: Atheneum.

Johns, J., & Lenski, S. (2005). *Improving reading: Strategies and resources* (4th ed.). Dubuque, IA: Kendall-Hunt.

Johnson, D. W., Johnson, R. T., & Holubec, E. J. (1988). *Cooperation in the classroom.* Edina, MN: Interaction Books.

Keller, D. (2004). *Applied learning.* Retrieved September 14, 2006, from http://www.newhorizons.org/strategies/applied_learning/keller.htm

Kennedy, M. (1995). *The Oxford dictionary of music.* New York: Oxford University Press.

Kinsey, L. C., & Moore, T. E. (2006). *Symmetry, shape, and space.* Emeryville, CA: Key College Press.

Lance, S., & Wolf, J. (2006). *The little blue book of advertising: 52 small ideas that can make a big difference.* New York: Portfolio Hardcover.

Lazear, D. (2003). *Eight ways of teaching: The artistry of teaching with multiple intelligences.* Thousand Oaks, CA: Corwin Press.

Learning, J. (2005). *The United States Constitution: What it says, what it means.* New York: Oxford University Press.

Levy, E., Holub, J., & Rosenblum, R. (1992). *If you were there when they signed the constitution.* New York: Scholastic.

Lozanov, G. (1978). *Suggestology and outlines of suggestology.* New York: Plenum.

MacLean, P. (1990). *The triune brain in evolution.* New York: Plenum.

Maestro, B. (1987). *A more perfect union: The story of our constitution.* New York: Lothrop, Lee and Shepard.

McTighe, J. (1996–97). What happens between assessments? *Educational Leadership, 54*(4), 6–12.

Mills, B. J. (2002). *Enhancing learning—and more!—through cooperative learning.* Retrieved September 19, 2006, from http://www.idea.ksu/edu

Moon, J. (2005). *Guide for busy academics no. 4: Learning through reflection.* Retrieved September 19, 2006, from http://www.heacademy.ac.uk

Morgan, N. (1995). *Chemistry in action: The molecules of everyday life.* New York: Oxford University Press.

O'Keefe, J., & Nadel, L. (1978). *The hippocampus as a cognitive map.* Oxford, UK: Clarendon.

Ornstein, R., & Sobel, D. (1987). *The healing brain and how it keeps us healthy.* New York: Simon & Schuster.

Pasachoff, N. (1996). *Marie Curie and the science of radioactivity.* New York: Oxford University Press.

Pert, C. (1997). *Molecules of emotion: Why you feel the way you feel.* New York: Scribner.

Peterson, B. (2004). *Understanding exposure: How to shoot great photographs with a film or digital camera.* New York: Amphoto Books.

Pinker, S. (1997). *How the mind works.* New York: W. W. Norton.

Posner, M. I., & Keele, S. W. (1973). Skill learning. In R. M. W. Travers (Ed.), *Second handbook of research on teaching* (pp. 122–183). Chicago: Rand McNally.

Prescott, J. (2005). *Music in the classroom.* Retrieved September 11, 2006, from http://teacher.scholastic.com/products/instructor/Jan05_music.htm

Pricken, M. (2004). *Creative advertising: Ideas and techniques from the world's best campaigns.* London: Thames & Hudson.

Prolman, M. (1995). *The constitution.* Danbury, CT: Children's Press.

Rauscher, F., Shaw, G. L., & Ky, K. N. (1993). Music and spatial task performance. *Nature, 365,* 611.

Rauscher, F., Shaw, G. L., & Ky, K. N. (1994). Brief intellectual gains sparked by classical music. *Brain-Mind Bulletin, 20*(5), 12–13.

Rauscher, F., Shaw, G. L., & Ky, K. N. (1997). Music training causes long-term enhancement of preschool children's spatial-temporal reasoning. *Neurological Research, 19*(2), 208.

Reagan, D., & Waide, R. (Eds.). (1996). *The food web of a tropical rain forest.* Chicago: University of Chicago Press.

Relf, P., & Degen, B. (1996). *The magic school bus gets eaten: A book about food chains.* New York: Scholastic.

Ross, A. (2006, September 4). Learning the score. *The New Yorker,* 82–88.

Rossotti, H. (1998). *Diverse atoms: Profiles of the chemical elements.* New York: Oxford University Press.

Silverstein, A., Silverstein, V. B., & Nunn, L. S. (1998). *Food chains.* Brookfield, CT: Twenty-First Century Books.

Spier, P. (1991). *We the people: The Constitution of the United States of America.* New York: Doubleday.

Sylwester, R. (1995). *A celebration of neurons: An educator's guide to the human brain.* Alexandria, VA: Association for Supervision and Curriculum Development.

Sylwester, R. (2002). *A biological brain in a cultural classroom: Applying biological research to classroom management* (2nd ed.). Thousand Oaks, CA: Corwin Press.

Sylwester, R. (2005). *How to explain a brain.* Thousand Oaks, CA: Corwin Press.

Sylwester, R. (2006a). *Is current schooling brain-based and brain-compatible? Part 2.* Retrieved August 17, 2006, from http://www.brainconnection.com

Sylwester, R. (2006b). *Mirror neuron update.* Retrieved August 17, 2006, from http://www.brainconnection.com

Tomlinson, C. A. (1999). *The differentiated classroom: Responding to the needs of all students.* Alexandria, VA: Association for Supervision and Curriculum Development.

Travis, C. (2006). *Constitution translated for kids.* Austin, TX: Synergy Books.

Value Based Management. (2006). *Kaizen.* Retrieved September 22, 2006, from http://www.valuebasedmanagement.net/methods_kaizen.html

Van Allsburg, C. (1981). *Jumanji.* Boston: Houghton Mifflin.

Warner, J. L. (producer), & Hunt, P. H. (director). (1972). *1776* [videotape]. United States: Columbia Pictures Corporation.

Wassman, R., & Rinsky, L. A. (1997). *Effective reading in a changing world* (2nd ed.). Upper Saddle River, NJ: Prentice-Hall.

Wegman, W. (1995). *Triangle, square, circle.* Westport, CT: Hyperion.

Wegman, W. (1998). *My town.* Westport, CT: Hyperion.

Wiggins, G., & McTighe, J. (2005). *Understanding by design* (expanded 2nd ed.). Alexandria, VA: Association for Supervision and Curriculum Development.

Wlodkowski, R. (1985). *Enhancing adult motivation to learn.* San Francisco: Jossey-Bass.

Woodson, R. D. (1996). *The complete idiot's guide to photography.* Indianapolis, IN: Alpha Books.

Zull, J. E. (2003). *What is "the art of changing the brain?"* Retrieved August 18, 2006, from http://www.newhorizons.org

Index

The Corwin Press logo—a raven striding across an open book—represents the union of courage and learning. Corwin Press is committed to improving education for all learners by publishing books and other professional development resources for those serving the field of PreK–12 education. By providing practical, hands-on materials, Corwin Press continues to carry out the promise of its motto: **"Helping Educators Do Their Work Better."**